Gospel Connections for Teens

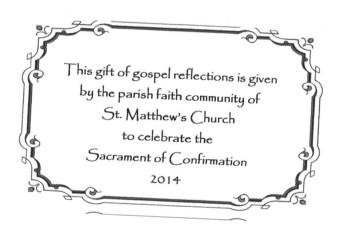

This gift of gospel reflections is given
by the parish faith community of
St. Matthew's Church
to celebrate the
Sacrament of Confirmation
2014

Gospel Connections for Teens

Reflections for Sunday Mass, Cycle A

Corey Brost, CSV

saint mary's press

The publishing team included Brian Singer-Towns, development editor; Lorraine Kilmartin, reviewer; prepress and manufacturing coordinated by the production departments of Saint Mary's Press.

Printed in the United States of America

3440

ISBN 978-0-88489-643-2

Library of Congress Cataloging-in-Publication Data

Brost, Corey.
    Gospel connections for teens : reflections for Sunday mass / Corey Brost.
        v. cm.
Contents: — [2] Cycle A.
ISBN 978-0-88489-643-2 (v. 3 : pbk.)
    1. Bible. N.T. Gospels—Meditations—Juvenile literature. 2. Church year meditations—Juvenile literature. I. Title.
BS2555.54.B76 2007
242'.63—dc22
                                                            2006000795

I dedicate this book to those who suffer injustice, especially those who are homeless or hungry, victims of domestic violence, trapped in war zones, unfairly imprisoned, or labeled as unpatriotic for challenging their government. May these Gospel passages and reflections inspire the young people who read them to stand by your side in the name of Christ, our savior.

This book was a joint effort. Three teens worked diligently as an editing team to help me refine each reflection. Their input was invaluable. So thanks to Rosanne Cruz, Dan Masterton, and Kate Schwarz. Your willingness to grow closer to Christ has inspired me.

Contents

Introduction

I wrote this book because I never had one like it when I was a teen. I struggled each Sunday to connect the Gospel to my teen ups and downs. I hope this book helps you make those connections.

First, a brief explanation. In the Church liturgical year, the Sunday Gospel readings follow a three-year cycle. This book covers the first year of that cycle, called cycle A. In cycle A most of the Gospel readings are taken from the Gospel of Matthew.

Here's how you use this book, then. Look at the chart that follows this introduction. Look up the date of the coming Sunday in the chart, and you will find the correct reflection. Commit to spending twenty minutes each week reflecting on the Gospel before you go to Mass. Use the book's reflection process or create your own. Then go to Mass on Sunday and compare your reflection to the homily. You might even want to get a few friends together over coffee or snacks during the week to compare thoughts on the readings.

Because of space limitations, I've edited a few lines out of some of the Gospel passages. The Scripture citations at the top of the page indicate the complete Gospel passage for that Sunday. If I've shortened the passage, you will see a second citation immediately following the passage, indicating the exact verses I used.

All but a few of the names in the reflections are made up, though all the people I mention are real people I've come across in life and ministry.

Reflection Chart

Sunday Gospel Reflection	Page No.	2007–2008	2010–2011	2013–2014
1st Sunday of Advent	14	Dec. 2	Nov. 28	Dec. 1
2nd Sunday of Advent	16	Dec. 9	Dec. 5	Dec. 8
3rd Sunday of Advent	18	Dec. 17	Dec. 12	Dec. 15
4th Sunday of Advent	20	Dec. 23	Dec. 19	Dec. 22
Christmas Day	22	Dec. 25	Dec. 25	Dec. 25
Holy Family	24	Dec. 30	Dec. 26	Dec. 29
Mary, Mother of God	26	Jan. 1	Jan. 1	Jan. 1
Epiphany Sunday	28	Jan. 6	Jan. 2	Jan. 5
Baptism of the Lord	30	Jan. 13	Jan. 9	Jan. 12
2nd Sunday in Ordinary Time	32	Jan. 20	Jan. 16	Jan. 19
3rd Sunday in Ordinary Time	34	Jan. 27	Jan. 23	Jan. 26
4th Sunday in Ordinary Time	36	Feb. 3	Jan. 30	Feb. 2
5th Sunday in Ordinary Time	38		Feb. 6	Feb. 9
6th Sunday in Ordinary Time	40		Feb. 13	Feb. 16
7th Sunday in Ordinary Time	42		Feb. 20	Feb. 23
8th Sunday in Ordinary Time	44		Feb. 27	Mar. 2
1st Sunday of Lent	46	Feb. 10	Mar. 13	Mar. 9
2nd Sunday of Lent	48	Feb. 17	Mar. 20	Mar. 16
3rd Sunday of Lent	50	Feb. 24	Mar. 27	Mar. 23
4th Sunday of Lent	52	Mar. 2	April 3	Mar. 30
5th Sunday of Lent	54	Mar. 9	April 10	April 6
Palm Sunday (The Passion)	56	Mar. 16	April 17	April 13
Easter Sunday	58	Mar. 23	April 24	April 20
2nd Sunday of Easter	60	Mar. 30	May 1	April 27
3rd Sunday of Easter	62	April 6	May 8	May 4
4th Sunday of Easter	64	April 13	May 15	May 11
5th Sunday of Easter	66	April 20	May 22	May 18
6th Sunday of Easter	68	April 27	May 29	May 25
7th Sunday of Easter	70	May 4	June 5	June 1

Reflections on the
Sunday Gospel Readings

First Sunday of Advent
Matthew 24:37–44

Jump on a Boat This Advent

Take :05 Examine

How did I live out last week's Gospel message? What was tough? What was rewarding?

Take :05 Read

Jesus said to his disciples: "As it was in the days of Noah, so it will be at the coming of the Son of Man. In those days before the flood, they were eating and drinking, marrying and giving in marriage, up to the day that Noah entered the ark. They did not know until the flood came and carried them all away. So will it be also at the coming of the Son of Man. Two men will be out in the field; one will be taken, and one will be left. Two women will be grinding at the mill; one will be taken, and one will be left. Therefore, stay awake! For you do not know on which day your Lord will come. Be sure of this: if the master of the house had known the hour of night when the thief was coming, he would have stayed awake and not let his house be broken into. So too, you also must be prepared, for at an hour you do not expect, the Son of Man will come."

Several years ago Hurricane Katrina flooded New Orleans. Hundreds died. Rescuers found hundreds trapped on rooftops. Some argued that many people suffered only because the government authorities weren't prepared for the storm.

As Advent begins this week, Jesus reminds us that people suffered in Noah's time because they weren't prepared. Remember the story? It tells us that sin and injustice— ignored by God's people—caused the world's destruction.

Are we ignoring sin and injustice today? This is a good season to think about that. As you do, prepare yourself for

Christ in three ways. First, take time this Advent to read newspapers closely. Look for evidence of injustice: war, poverty, prejudice. Keep your eyes open at school. Notice kids ignored by others and notice the bullies who prey on the weak.

Sadly, you'll see that our world is still plagued by sin and injustice.

But remember, Advent is also a season of hope. It comes at the darkest time of the year (at least in the Northern Hemisphere), so we light candles to remember that Christ's power seeks to beat back the darkness of injustice every day.

Second, prepare yourself by looking for evidence of grace. To every war, God sends peacemakers. To every kid who feels left out, God sends a friend. Stay awake, Jesus says, and you'll see reasons for hope all over the world.

Third, prepare yourself to be grace and hope this season, the person who shines light by standing for peace, feeding the hungry, forgiving an enemy, or welcoming an outcast.

Sure, sin floods our world, but God sends boats to the rescue. Jump on board this Advent. People stranded by pain and injustice are waiting for you.

Take :10 Reflect

If a word or phrase from the Gospel grabs your heart, sit quietly for several minutes, repeating it to yourself and asking God to show you how it applies to your life. Or, reflect and possibly journal on the following question:

- Where can you make a difference at home, at school, or in the world this Advent?

Don't Just Trim the Tree

Take :05 Examine

How did I live out last week's Gospel message? What was tough? What was rewarding?

Take :05 Read

John the Baptist appeared, preaching in the desert of Judea and saying, "Repent, for the kingdom of heaven is at hand!" It was of him that the prophet Isaiah had spoken when he said:

> *A voice of one crying out in the desert,*
> *Prepare the way of the Lord,*
> > *make straight his paths.*

John wore clothing made of camel's hair and had a leather belt around his waist. His food was locusts and wild honey. At that time Jerusalem, all Judea, and the whole region around the Jordan were going out to him and were being baptized by him in the Jordan River as they acknowledged their sins.

When he saw many of the Pharisees and Sadducees coming to his baptism, he said to them, "You brood of vipers! Who warned you to flee from the coming wrath? Produce good fruit as evidence of your repentance. And do not presume to say to yourselves, 'We have Abraham as our father.' For I tell you, God can raise up children to Abraham from these stones. Even now the ax lies at the root of the trees. Therefore every tree that does not bear good fruit will be cut down and thrown into the fire."
(Matthew 3:1–10)

Maybe this Advent we should trim and burn some tree limbs, not just trim our Christmas trees.

John the Baptist seems to sternly warn religious leaders that people who ignore his call to change will face a fiery judgment. They'll be like rotten trees cut down and burned.

I think John liked to shock people. But for good reason. He lived in a world full of poverty and injustice. He wanted people to face how their sins were hurting the world.

Don't let John's harsh words scare you. True, our sinful habits and attitudes are like rotten trees or bare branches. Things like selfishness and prejudice take away our happiness, hurt others, and keep us from working for a just world. But Jesus can help us trim these "tree limbs" from our lives. I know a young man who decided as a teen to change his life in the van ride home from a Christian conference. He hadn't been treating girls he'd dated with respect. He'd been hanging out with the wrong crowd. Jesus, he said, showed him what to change and gave him the confidence to do it. He's a lot happier now.

We light candles in Advent to remember that Christ can bring light (guidance and warmth) to the darkness in our lives and in the world. We also remember that Christ's light can burn away what holds us back from our full potential. Take time in Advent to feel God's compassion in the sacrament of Penance and Reconciliation. Or talk with a teacher, friend, or parent about things you'd like to change.

You'll realize, as you trim your Christmas tree, that Jesus is gently trimming your soul.

Take :10 Reflect

If a word or phrase from the Gospel grabs your heart, sit quietly for several minutes, repeating it to yourself and asking God to show you how it applies to your life. Or, reflect and possibly journal on the following question:

- What can you change about yourself this Advent to make the world a brighter place?

Is Jesus "the One" for You?

Take :05 Examine

How did I live out last week's Gospel message? What was tough? What was rewarding?

Take :05 Read

When John the Baptist heard in prison of the works of the Christ, he sent his disciples to Jesus with this question, "Are you the one who is to come, or should we look for another?" Jesus said to them in reply, "Go and tell John what you hear and see: the blind regain their sight, the lame walk, lepers are cleansed, the deaf hear, the dead are raised, and the poor have the good news proclaimed to them. And blessed is the one who takes no offense at me." (Matthew 11:2–6)

Is Jesus really "the One"?

The answer for this guy I knew was no.

This guy really wanted fame and status. He wanted a big bankroll and all the stuff that comes with it. He wanted popularity. He was, after all, a bartender at a popular bar.

Clearly Jesus wasn't the One for him. Following Jesus just doesn't guarantee all those things.

John the Baptist had his doubts too, according to this week's Gospel. But John was looking for different things. He hungered for a world where people opened their eyes to injustice, where people disabled by disease or poverty could live with dignity, where each person lived to spread God's message of peace. Look around, Jesus told John's followers, and give John hope by telling him about the world I'm creating and teaching others to create.

How about you this Advent? Is Jesus the One for you? It will depend on what you are looking for in life. He is the

One for a lot of young people I know and have taught, including Frank, who proclaims the Good News to the poor by teaching in a poor part of Los Angeles. He is the One for Cynthia, who gives sight to the blind by leading youth group discussions about faith and morals at her parish. He is the One for Bob, who opens people's ears to God's word by cantoring each Sunday at Mass. If you hunger for the same world John the Baptist hoped to create, and if you hunger to live a meaningful life, then Jesus is the One for you.

Do other hungers tempt you away from Jesus? As humans we can forget how much Jesus offers and chase after money, beauty, status, and popularity. I know. The bartender at the beginning of the reflection? That was me! I wasted a lot of time before deciding Jesus is the One for me. But he took me back and showed me how to make life meaningful.

If you've been chasing after the wrong things, use this Advent to recommit yourself to Jesus and his mission. If you still have your doubts, that's okay. Just ask Jesus to clear them up. John the Baptist did.

Take :10 Reflect

If a word or phrase from the Gospel grabs your heart, sit quietly for several minutes, repeating it to yourself and asking God to show you how it applies to your life. Or, reflect and possibly journal on the following questions:

- How can following Jesus make your life more meaningful and help you change the world? What doubts do you have about committing yourself to him?

Here's a Real Man

Take :05 Examine

How did I live out last week's Gospel message? What was tough? What was rewarding?

Take :05 Read

This is how the birth of Jesus Christ came about. When his mother Mary was betrothed to Joseph, but before they lived together, she was found with child through the Holy Spirit. Joseph her husband, since he was a righteous man, yet unwilling to expose her to shame, decided to divorce her quietly. Such was his intention when, behold, the angel of the Lord appeared to him in a dream and said, "Joseph, son of David, do not be afraid to take Mary your wife into your home. For it is through the Holy Spirit that this child has been conceived in her. She will bear a son and you are to name him Jesus, because he will save his people from their sins." All this took place to fulfill what the Lord had said through the prophet:

Behold, the virgin shall conceive and bear a son
and they shall name him Emmanuel,

which means "God is with us." When Joseph awoke, he did as the angel of the Lord had commanded him and took his wife into his home.

Not too long ago, I led a wake service for a teen shot in the back by two other teens. Apparently, the two young men who killed José thought real men settle arguments by grabbing guns.

How sad, and it seems all too common in our nation. Young men kill each other to prove their "manliness."

Other men—young and old—beat women or use them sexually and brag about it later.

Man, does our culture need Saint Joseph as a role model! Here was a real man. His fiancée turned up pregnant, which would have caused him public shame in ancient Israel. Under the law he had the right to avenge that shame by leaving her or even requesting that she be put to death. But the Gospel tells us he instead chose to divorce her quietly.

And the story goes on. He believed God was telling him to accept Mary because she was pregnant by the Holy Spirit. He could have heard and accepted that only if he was a man who prayed regularly and practiced his Jewish faith.

Joseph: a man of peace who respected women in a culture that treated them as property; a man of prayer able to hear and courageously follow God's call—even though he risked public humiliation.

Don't we need more men like that today? How different would our schools be if more young men reached out to kids who are put down? if more young men saw dating as a way to make a friend, not to notch a sexual victory? How different would our neighborhoods be if more young men stood up for themselves without resorting to violence?

If you're a guy, ask Saint Joseph for guidance this Advent. If you're a girl, challenge your male friends to be "real men"—like Mary's husband.

Take :10 Reflect

If a word or phrase from the Gospel grabs your heart, sit quietly for several minutes, repeating it to yourself and asking God to show you how it applies to your life. Or, reflect and possibly journal on the following question:

- Which men in your life show the qualities Saint Joseph had?

Don't Be Afraid of the Dark

Take :05 Examine

How did I live out last week's Gospel message? What was tough? What was rewarding?

Take :05 Read

In the beginning was the Word,
  and the Word was with God,
  and the Word was God.
He was in the beginning with God.
All things came to be through him,
  and without him nothing came to be.
What came to be through him was life,
  and this life was the light of the human race;
  the light shines in the darkness,
  and the darkness has not overcome it.
The true light, which enlightens everyone, was coming into the world.
  He was in the world,
  and the world came to be through him,
  but the world did not know him.
He came to what was his own,
  but his own people did not accept him.

But to those who did accept him he gave power to become children of God, to those who believe in his name, who were born not by natural generation nor by human choice nor by a man's decision but of God.
  And the Word became flesh
  and made his dwelling among us,
  and we saw his glory,
  the glory as of the Father's only Son,
  full of grace and truth.

Fights with friends. Conflicts with parents. Struggles for grades. Fear of failure. Loneliness. Gangs and violence. So many things can beat us down and darken our days.

Thank God Christmas Day reminds us that nothing can overcome us because Jesus, God's promise of hope, came into our world. Christ's light can calm our darkest fears and guide us through overwhelming problems. Christ's strength and peace can fill us if we face rejection for doing the right thing. Remember, Christ also faced those things that beat us down, especially rejection, conflict, and loneliness.

But this isn't automatic. We must choose to let Christ's light in. Pray daily. Take at least fifteen minutes each morning or night to talk with Jesus. Or just sit quietly, imagining him with you. Follow Jesus' life in the Sunday Gospel readings. Take twenty minutes each week to read the Sunday Gospel and think about what it offers your life. Compare the priest's homily to what you think is important.

Learn to live like Jesus. Make your life an example of hope and goodness for others. Apologize when you hurt someone. Be patient with your Christian growth. Share your Christian successes and failures with people you trust. Reach out to fellow Christians—adults and teens—for Christ's love when times get dark. Ask them to help you find Christ when God seems hard to find.

The world changed when Jesus entered it. Fear and despair lost their power. Remember, when times get tough, you can bask in "the true light."

Take :10 Reflect

If a word or phrase from the Gospel grabs your heart, sit quietly for several minutes, repeating it to yourself and asking God to show you how it applies to your life. Or, reflect and possibly journal on the following question:

- Where do you need Christ's light, or where can you offer his light right now?

God Still Makes Families Holy

Take :05 Examine

How did I live out last week's Gospel message? What was
tough? What was rewarding?

Take :05 Read

*When the magi had departed, behold, the angel of the Lord
appeared to Joseph in a dream and said, "Rise, take the child
and his mother, flee to Egypt, and stay there until I tell you.
Herod is going to search for the child to destroy him." Joseph
rose and took the child and his mother by night and departed
for Egypt. He stayed there until the death of Herod, that what
the Lord had said through the prophet might be fulfilled, Out of
Egypt I called my son.*

*When Herod had died, behold, the angel of the Lord appeared
in a dream to Joseph in Egypt and said, "Rise, take the child and
his mother and go to the land of Israel, for those who sought the
child's life are dead." He rose, took the child and his mother, and
went to the land of Israel. But when he heard that Archelaus was
ruling over Judea in place of his father Herod, he was afraid to
go back there. And because he had been warned in a dream, he
departed for the region of Galilee. He went and dwelt in a town
called Nazareth, so that what had been spoken through the
prophets might be fulfilled, He shall be called a Nazorean.*

Two families. One went for a week to Mexico, helped care
for orphans and build a church. The other has a dad recov-
ering from alcoholism, who helped his nephew recover
from cocaine addiction by taking the nephew to AA meetings.

Those are "holy families."

Scripture scholars say that in this week's Gospel, Matthew was probably comparing Jesus to Moses, who also spent time in Egypt. Jesus, like Moses, knew God liberates. God liberated the Israelites from slavery. Jesus liberated us from slavery to sin by his death and Resurrection. We use Jesus' liberating power when we draw close to him and help those who suffer.

The two families above, like the Holy Family of Joseph, Mary, and Jesus, spread God's liberating power. One family helped free people from poverty by serving them. The father in the other family helped free his nephew from drugs by guiding him. Many other families are like them. Some pray together, visit soup kitchens, or attend family retreats.

Is your family spreading God's liberating power? Does a member of your family need freedom from something like addiction, fear, or sadness? Talk about this with a parent or another trusted Christian adult this week.

If you can, thank God this week for how God takes care of you through your family. This might be hard for some young people because of alcoholism, domestic abuse, or divorce. If that's you, talk this week with an adult Christian about where you can find help. God will guide you to liberation, as well.

Take :10 Reflect

If a word or phrase from the Gospel grabs your heart, sit quietly for several minutes, repeating it to yourself and asking God to show you how it applies to your life. Or, reflect and possibly journal on the following question:

- What could you do to make your family more "holy" or to seek God's help with your family problems?

Mary, Mother of God
Luke 2:16–21

Get Schooled by Today's Shepherds

How did I live out last week's Gospel message? What was tough? What was rewarding?

The shepherds went in haste to Bethlehem and found Mary and Joseph, and the infant lying in the manger. When they saw this, they made known the message that had been told them about this child. All who heard it were amazed by what had been told them by the shepherds. And Mary kept all these things, reflecting on them in her heart. Then the shepherds returned, glorifying and praising God for all they had heard and seen, just as it had been told to them.

When eight days were completed for his circumcision, he was named Jesus, the name given him by the angel before he was conceived in the womb.

Bob wasn't sure what God wanted from him, so he asked me one day how my campus ministry office could help him figure it out.

I took him to a soup kitchen.

It was the first of many trips for him. Eventually, at our high school, he helped start a ministry to homeless people that allowed him also to meet and talk with folks who lived on the streets. He continued service like this through college. He found talents he never thought he had. He learned things about life he never thought he'd learn. His faith grew. Now Bob still serves homeless people while also teaching other Catholics how they can find meaning by serving people rejected by others.

He reminds me of Mary. This Gospel says the shepherds "amazed" Mary with their message. Like today's poor and homeless people, shepherds were rejected by many people. Mary was different. She listened to their insights and then reflected on them "in her heart." Maybe their story reminded her about the special nature of her son—and her mission in his life.

We can learn from Mary and Bob. God has a mission for each of us. Sometimes it's hard to discover. Sometimes we think it's crazy to think God needs us. That's why serving people rejected by others is critical. Service helps you discover your talents and build your confidence—even when it's hard to believe in yourself. And the folks you meet will offer you valuable insight into life and faith. Like Bob, if you spend time serving and learning from people rejected by others—the poor, the sick, the forgotten, the lonely kids at school—you'll find direction for yourself and strength for your faith.

Learn from Bob this new year. Be open to what people who are rejected by others have to show you. You might be amazed like Mary. You'll discover that God needs and values you just as much as he needed her.

Take :10 Reflect

If a word or phrase from the Gospel grabs your heart, sit quietly for several minutes, repeating it to yourself and asking God to show you how it applies to your life. Or, reflect and possibly journal on the following questions:

- Where in my community could I go to serve and learn from people rejected by others? What talents do I have that could help there?

The Magi Would Come to Your House Too

Take :05 Examine

How did I live out last week's Gospel message? What was tough? What was rewarding?

Take :05 Read

When Jesus was born in Bethlehem of Judea, in the days of King Herod, behold, magi from the east arrived in Jerusalem, saying, "Where is the newborn king of the Jews? We saw his star at its rising and have come to do him homage." When King Herod heard this, he was greatly troubled, and all Jerusalem with him. . . . He sent them to Bethlehem and said, "Go and search diligently for the child. When you have found him, bring me word, that I too may go and do him homage." After their audience with the king they set out. And behold, the star that they had seen at its rising preceded them, until it came and stopped over the place where the child was. They were overjoyed at seeing the star, and on entering the house they saw the child with Mary his mother. They prostrated themselves and did him homage. Then they opened their treasures and offered him gifts of gold, frankincense, and myrrh. And having been warned in a dream not to return to Herod, they departed for their country by another way. (Matthew 2:1–3,8–12)

I know high school students who recently spent a Sunday at a peace rally, helping set up displays showing the horror of the war in Iraq and listening to speakers talk about our call to be peacemakers. They are part of a high school group that explores ways teens can stand against violence and oppression. They aren't waiting for someone else to do something. They know they have the power to make a difference.

They remind me of the message from this week's Gospel. Scripture scholars say the biblical Magi were high-ranking advisers to rulers of powerful countries east of Israel. Yet these Magi realized that the true king was born in a small village in an insignificant country. Matthew tells this story to show us how God works to heal the world through the people we don't see as powerful—like a child born in a manger. Too often people wait for politicians to end poverty, war, or abortion. But we can help craft solutions to those problems with our heads and hearts.

We must not lack confidence or see ourselves as powerless. Believe that God can use you to make a difference. Concerned about child sweatshops? Then organize friends to boycott clothes made by kids—especially if those clothes have your school name on them. Want to stop abortion? Help out at an agency that supports unwed mothers.

The Magi were wise. They knew that God uses people others see as powerless to do great things. Remember their wisdom when you feel powerless.

Take :10 Reflect

If a word or phrase from the Gospel grabs your heart, sit quietly for several minutes, repeating it to yourself and asking God to show you how it applies to your life. Or, reflect and possibly journal on the following questions:

- When I look around at the world's problems, where could you make a difference? What steps can you take to get started this week?

Jesus Needed Tutoring?

Take :05 Examine

How did I live out last week's Gospel message? What was tough? What was rewarding?

Take :05 Read

Jesus came from Galilee to John at the Jordan to be baptized by him. John tried to prevent him, saying, "I need to be baptized by you, and yet you are coming to me?" Jesus said to him in reply, "Allow it now, for thus it is fitting for us to fulfill all righteousness." Then he allowed him. After Jesus was baptized, he came up from the water and behold, the heavens were opened for him, and he saw the Spirit of God descending like a dove and coming upon him. And a voice came from the heavens, saying, "This is my beloved Son, with whom I am well pleased."

José wasn't sure which direction to follow when he was in high school. But one thing was sure, this guy Miguel sure had a direction for him.

Miguel kept inviting him to the parish youth group meeting. Sometimes José would go. During the meetings Miguel would always invite him to let the Gospel of Christ direct him. Always friendly and encouraging, with a good sense of humor, Miguel showed his faith by treating others with respect and compassion. He also told stories about how Jesus made a difference in his life.

Eventually Miguel's love for Christ—which he showed through his actions and words—convinced José. One day José decided to redirect his life. The Gospel would be his guide too.

José's life changed for the better because Miguel decided to take him under his wing and show him—through words and deeds—how God could make a difference for him.

John the Baptist did the same thing for Jesus, some Scripture scholars say. They think Jesus may have followed John the Baptist before be began his own ministry. Maybe John helped Jesus discover his talents and mission. Maybe he took Jesus by the hand and trained him for ministry. One thing is sure. When Herod arrested John, Jesus started his ministry, using the talents he developed under his mentor.

How about you? Who has shown you how to live as a Christian and why it's worthwhile? Can you thank him or her this week? Can you thank God for that person's presence in your life?

How about the people—older and younger—who look to you as a role model or could benefit from your guidance? Can you make even more of an effort to guide them and show them through your actions how to live like a Christian?

Now José has picked up where Miguel left off. He leads the youth group that Miguel once led. Even though Miguel has moved on, God's Spirit keeps working.

Take :10 Reflect

If a word or phrase from the Gospel grabs your heart, sit quietly for several minutes, repeating it to yourself and asking God to show you how it applies to your life. Or, reflect and possibly journal on the following questions:

- Who sees you as a Christian role model? How could you be an even stronger role model?

Who Are You Pointing At?

Take :05 Examine

How did I live out last week's Gospel message? What was tough? What was rewarding?

Take :05 Read

John the Baptist saw Jesus coming toward him and said, "Behold, the Lamb of God, who takes away the sin of the world. He is the one of whom I said, 'A man is coming after me who ranks ahead of me because he existed before me.' I did not know him, but the reason why I came baptizing with water was that he might be made known to Israel." John testified further, saying, "I saw the Spirit come down like a dove from heaven and remain upon him. I did not know him, but the one who sent me to baptize with water told me, 'On whomever you see the Spirit come down and remain, he is the one who will baptize with the Holy Spirit.' Now I have seen and testified that he is the Son of God."

Mark always loved rap.

When he was younger, he really followed where some rap songs pointed him—toward money and respect. Unfortunately, he found his money by selling drugs. He earned his respect by gangbanging. Meanwhile, he knew some friends from his church who pointed in a different direction. Jesus and the Gospel, they kept arguing, would bring him everything he really wanted.

He now thanks God and those parishioners who kept hounding him to hang out with them. Over time he realized he was headed for prison or an early grave. So he looked where they pointed—toward Jesus.

Now Mark uses his love of rap to point others toward Jesus. He and a friend have written rhymes that tell about their mistakes and their search for meaning. They look for churches where they can invite teens to hear their rap. Mark is like John in this week's Gospel. He keeps pointing others toward the Lord, because he knows Jesus is the answer for people's hopes and dreams.

Where do our lives point? Each day, through each action, we point toward something. Do we point toward Jesus by forgiving others and ourselves, admitting our mistakes, standing for peace, serving the people rejected by others, talking openly about faith, and doing what's right when that's tough to do? Do people look at us and consider following Jesus because they see how worthwhile discipleship is for us?

Don't think you have to be perfect. The best Christian witnesses are people like Mark—imperfect people who show others how to learn from mistakes and start over. Take a moment this week and look at your actions. Be patient with yourself. Believe in yourself. Like the people in Mark's church, your witness might save someone from making mistakes that could end in jail or the cemetery.

So, who are you pointing at?

Take :10 Reflect

If a word or phrase from the Gospel grabs your heart, sit quietly for several minutes, repeating it to yourself and asking God to show you how it applies to your life. Or, reflect and possibly journal on the following question:

* Who in your life reminds you of John the Baptist, because his or her words and actions point toward Jesus?

Let God Use Tragedy for Good

Take :05 Examine

How did I live out last week's Gospel message? What was tough? What was rewarding?

Take :05 Read

When Jesus heard that John had been arrested, he withdrew to Galilee. He left Nazareth and went to live in Capernaum by the sea, in the region of Zebulun and Naphtali, that what had been said through Isaiah the prophet might be fulfilled:

Land of Zebulun and land of Naphtali,
>the way to the sea, beyond the Jordan,
>Galilee of the Gentiles,
the people who sit in darkness
>have seen a great light,
on those dwelling in a land overshadowed by death
>light has arisen.

From that time on, Jesus began to preach and say, "Repent, for the kingdom of heaven is at hand." (Matthew 4:12–17)

What went through Jesus' mind when they arrested John?

Remember, John and Jesus were close. Herod, who arrested John, was a cruel tyrant. Jesus must have realized John was facing torture and a brutal death. The Gospel makes it sound like Jesus withdrew for prayer and reflection. Did he reconsider dedicating his life to God? Did he need to grieve? Was he afraid? Did he consider seeking revenge? No one is sure why he withdrew, but it must have been a tough time for him.

The Gospel also says that John's arrest marked the beginning of Jesus' ministry. So he withdrew but then decided God was calling him to start his own ministry to replace John's.

How do you deal with tragedy and loss? It seems that Jesus responded by starting his own ministry to announce God's Reign of peace. Too often today it seems that people respond to tragedy with destructive options. Some lash out at others or use alcohol or other drugs to numb the pain. Some give up.

Follow Jesus' example. God doesn't bring tragedy into your life, but God certainly wants to help you deal with it or learn from it. Prayer and discussions with other Christians will help you hang in there during tough times or learn how to avoid them in the future. Write letters to God in a private journal. Learn to meditate. Like Jesus, you will find that wisdom or even a new direction for your life comes from a tragedy.

Here's a good example. I know students whose mothers have suffered with breast cancer. But they have let that tragedy motivate them to improve the lives of others. They are doing that by educating others about breast cancer and raising money to help find a cure. Like Jesus, they suffered painful tragedy, but they let the tragedy—with the help of God—guide them in acting to make the world a better place.

Take :10 Reflect

If a word or phrase from the Gospel grabs your heart, sit quietly for several minutes, repeating it to yourself and asking God to show you how it applies to your life. Or, reflect and possibly journal on the following questions:

- In what specific ways could teens let God help them through tragedy? Do you know people who have responded to tragedy by using their experiences to help others?

Take a Risk

Take :05 Examine

How did I live out last week's Gospel message? What was tough? What was rewarding?

Take :05 Read

When Jesus saw the crowds, he went up the mountain, and after he had sat down, his disciples came to him. He began to teach them, saying:
"Blessed are the poor in spirit,
*   for theirs is the kingdom of heaven.*
* Blessed are they who mourn,*
*   for they will be comforted.*
* Blessed are the meek,*
*   for they will inherit the land.*
* Blessed are they who hunger and thirst for righteousness,*
*   for they will be satisfied.*
* Blessed are the merciful,*
*   for they will be shown mercy.*
* Blessed are the clean of heart,*
*   for they will see God.*
* Blessed are the peacemakers,*
*   for they will be called children of God.*
* Blessed are they who are persecuted for the sake of*
*   righteousness,*
*   for theirs is the kingdom of heaven.*
Blessed are you when they insult you and persecute you and utter every kind of evil against you falsely because of me. Rejoice and be glad, for your reward will be great in heaven."

I was driving teens in a van once when I jokingly threatened to tie a loud kid to the roof with a cord. That way, I joked, he could still travel with us but we wouldn't have to listen to him.

His response? "That would be cool." And he probably would have enjoyed it.

Yep, teens like risk. Rock climbing. Driving fast. The rush of adrenalin. The thrill of adventure.

That's why teens make excellent disciples. Following Jesus is all about risk. In this week's Gospel, Jesus calls his disciples to risk. The Beatitudes (which is what we call the list in this Gospel) are risky actions Jesus tells his followers to choose. For example, be poor in spirit. (Ask God's guidance for all decisions). Be meek. (Treat others as if they're more important than you.) Mourn. (Don't hide your pain.) Be merciful. (Choose forgiveness.) Be a peacemaker. (Work publicly for peace and justice.)

You take a risk when you live a Beatitude. People might mock you for letting God, rather than wealth or popularity, set your direction. People might put you down when someone hurts you and you don't get even. People might call you crazy for protesting war.

But Jesus says God will bless us when we take these risks. In other words, God will act in our favor. So when you let God direct you, God will give you a meaningful life. When you face your pain and mourn, God will comfort you through prayer or by sending people to help you. When you choose mercy and work for peace, God will give you the strength you need to forgive and the courage to stand publicly against violence.

So take a risk this week. Live the Beatitudes. It's an adventure.

Take :10 Reflect

If a word or phrase from the Gospel grabs your heart, sit quietly for several minutes, repeating it to yourself and asking God to show you how it applies to your life. Or, reflect and possibly journal on the following questions:

- Which Beatitude seems the riskiest for you to live? Which seems the easiest?

Be a Fire Starter

Take :05 Examine

How did I live out last week's Gospel message? What was tough? What was rewarding?

Take :05 Read

Jesus said to his disciples: "You are the salt of the earth. But if salt loses its taste, with what can it be seasoned? It is no longer good for anything but to be thrown out and trampled underfoot. You are the light of the world. A city set on a mountain cannot be hidden. Nor do they light a lamp and then put it under a bushel basket; it is set on a lampstand, where it gives light to all in the house. Just so, your light must shine before others, that they may see your good deeds and glorify your heavenly Father."

"From now on," the teen girl said, "I'm not going to be silent when I hear an ethnic joke."

She was one of twenty-seven teens on a retreat about the Christian response to ethnic prejudice. Many of the white teens were moved as black and Latino teens talked about the pain of ethnic bias. Many of the black and Latino teens felt hopeful because the white teens listened with open hearts.

The twenty-four hours they spent talking, laughing, and praying together changed many teens on the retreat. It energized them to go home and make a difference in their families and schools. They realized Jesus was right. They really can be salt and light.

Jesus has faith in his disciples. He knows that like light, they can provide warmth and guidance to the world. And he believes that like salt—which scholars say families used to start cooking fires—his disciples can ignite changes in society.

Jesus has that same faith in you, even though you might not believe it at times. Within you lies the power to guide and warm people, as well as the power to motivate others to change themselves and the world. Retreats are great opportunities to become aware of that. An intense time of discussion and prayer with other teens and adults can show you how much faith God really has in you.

Remember the retreat about prejudice? A group of teens started it after they attended a conference that challenged them to be salt and light. They left the conference believing in themselves. They sought guidance from some adults and, as a result, have helped create a retreat program that makes a difference in a serious social issue. The teens they influence are now light and salt for other teens. See how it all works?

Look for opportunities like retreats and Christian conferences. Let Jesus remind you how much you have to offer. You'll be amazed at the power you have within yourself.

Take :10 Reflect

If a word or phrase from the Gospel grabs your heart, sit quietly for several minutes, repeating it to yourself and asking God to show you how it applies to your life. Or, reflect and possibly journal on the following question:

- When was a time when you or someone you know really made a difference after going on a retreat or some other spiritual event?

Thoughts Do Count

Take :05 Examine

How did I live out last week's Gospel message? What was tough? What was rewarding?

Take :05 Read

Jesus said to his disciples: "I tell you, unless your righteousness surpasses that of the scribes and Pharisees, you will not enter the kingdom of heaven.

"You have heard that it was said to your ancestors, You shall not kill; and whoever kills will be liable to judgment. But I say to you, whoever is angry with his brother will be liable to judgment.

"You have heard that it was said, You shall not commit adultery. But I say to you, everyone who looks at a woman with lust has already committed adultery with her in his heart.

"Again you have heard that it was said to your ancestors, Do not take a false oath, but make good to the Lord all that you vow. But I say to you, do not swear at all. Let your 'Yes' mean 'Yes,' and your 'No' mean 'No.' Anything more is from the evil one."
(Matthew 5:20–22a,27–28,33–34a,37)

I remember a sad day in my high school ministry. I learned that a group of senior boys had started a betting pool to see which one could have sex with the most freshman girls. I couldn't believe the guys could care so little about these girls. They saw them as playthings to manipulate for sex, not as people with hopes, dreams, and feelings.

Clearly that betting pool represented serious sin— regardless of whether any boy ever touched a girl. It's the thought that counts. And that's Jesus' point in this week's Gospel.

We might think we hurt people only if we actually *do* something to them. Not true. We hurt people and ourselves when we nurture thoughts that belittle or dehumanize those people.

God knows it's hard for us to control our thinking. It's easy to feed on our anger against or lust for another person. But that way of thinking can make us forget that God calls us to forgive our enemies and treat each person with respect. The more we feed angry or lustful thoughts, the more likely we are to act on them.

Here's some advice. Nonviolently confront the people who hurt you. Express your feelings without attacking those people or seeking vengeance. That will help you stop replaying the hurt in your mind. Sexual feelings are normal. Don't be ashamed of them. But always remind yourself that the people who spark them are God's children, not objects of pleasure. And when you feel stuck in lust or anger, pray for that person. God will change your perspective. Finally, talk with an adult you trust if you can't free yourself from lustful or vengeful thinking.

Remember, when it comes to others, the thoughts do count.

Take :10 Reflect

If a word or phrase from the Gospel grabs your heart, sit quietly for several minutes, repeating it to yourself and asking God to show you how it applies to your life. Or, reflect and possibly journal on the following question:

• What strategies would you propose to teens who struggle with feelings of anger or lust?

Break the Cycle

Take :05 Examine

How did I live out last week's Gospel message? What was tough? What was rewarding?

Take :05 Read

Jesus said to his disciples:"You have heard that it was said, An eye for an eye and a tooth for a tooth. But I say to you, offer no resistance to one who is evil. When someone strikes you on your right cheek, turn the other one as well. If anyone wants to go to law with you over your tunic, hand over your cloak as well. Should anyone press you into service for one mile, go for two miles. Give to the one who asks of you, and do not turn your back on one who wants to borrow.

"You have heard that it was said, You shall love your neighbor and hate your enemy. But I say to you, love your enemies and pray for those who persecute you, that you may be children of your heavenly Father, for he makes his sun rise on the bad and the good, and causes rain to fall on the just and the unjust. For if you love those who love you, what recompense will you have? Do not the tax collectors do the same? And if you greet your brothers only, what is unusual about that? Do not the pagans do the same? So be perfect, just as your heavenly Father is perfect."

Here are two young men who broke the cycle of greed and violence that hurts our nation.

Frank's friend died in gang violence. Frank's friends kept urging him to get revenge. But he looked to God for help. He spent a lot of time at church and with adult church leaders as he struggled with anger and grief. That helped him break the cycle of violence by choosing against revenge.

Bob lives in a wealthy community where many teens drive expensive cars and live in expensive homes. Talk at his school often focuses on the newest games, computers, and clothes. But Bob found his meaning by helping out at a local soup kitchen, not by buying more and more for himself. He eventually helped lead service trips for other teens. He broke the cycle of greed and selfishness that traps many people in wealthy towns.

Frank and Bob put this week's Gospel into practice. Jesus challenges his disciples to break the cycles of sin that suck so many people in and cause so much destruction in the world. Turn the other cheek. That means standing up for your rights without resorting to violence or seeking revenge. Jesus also tells us to sacrifice time and money for the needs of all people, even for our enemies. These are tough teachings. But our world hurts. Practicing violence, revenge, and greed hasn't made things better. Maybe it is time to try Jesus' way.

Many teens today—like Frank and Bob—take Jesus' challenges and ask God for the strength to meet them. Will you?

Take :10 Reflect

If a word or phrase from the Gospel grabs your heart, sit quietly for several minutes, repeating it to yourself and asking God to show you how it applies to your life. Or, reflect and possibly journal on the following question:

- How in your family, school, or community could you break a cycle of violence, revenge, or greed?

Seek First . . . the Best College?

Take :05 Examine

How did I live out last week's Gospel message? What was tough? What was rewarding?

Take :05 Read

Jesus said to his disciples: "No one can serve two masters. He will either hate one and love the other, or be devoted to one and despise the other. You cannot serve God and mammon.

"Therefore I tell you, do not worry about your life, what you will eat or drink, or about your body, what you will wear. Is not life more than food and the body more than clothing? . . . But seek first the kingdom of God and his righteousness, and all these things will be given you besides. Do not worry about tomorrow; tomorrow will take care of itself. Sufficient for a day is its own evil." (Matthew 6:24–25, 33–34)

Dishonesty. It plagues our high schools. Many students will do anything to get ahead. Some teachers go crazy trying to develop ways to stop cheating. Others are heartbroken when students they respect justify academic dishonesty.

And Jesus said, "Seek first . . . the highest grade, the best college. . . ." Uh, not exactly.

I worked many years in Catholic high schools. I worry about the pressure students feel to be number one.

Here is the message many students pick up: "I have to get the highest grades and be in the most activities—otherwise I won't get into the best college. If I don't get into the best college, I will be a failure." Too often, even well-meaning parents and guidance counselors feed that message.

That message can devastate young people. It leads some to justify dishonesty. It leads others to use alcohol and other drugs. It leads others to experience depression and despair.

If you've heard that message, let me offer a different one—one from the God who will always be with you. "Seek first the kingdom of God, and all these things will follow." Here's how you do that. Develop your character. Honesty, compassion, and generosity will make your life more meaningful than the highest grades, longest résumé, or best college. Develop your prayer life. Using daily personal prayer and attending weekly Mass will remind you that God's love and protection don't depend on personal success. Build time into your schedule for service. That reminds you that you don't need a high ACT or SAT score to make a difference in the world and feel good about yourself.

Sure, work hard in school. Develop your brain and body through activities. But remember, almost any school can prepare you well for a career if you work hard. Also remember, our world needs more people with Christian character, not more millionaires.

Take :10 Reflect

If a word or phrase from the Gospel grabs your heart, sit quietly for several minutes, repeating it to yourself and asking God to show you how it applies to your life. Or, reflect and possibly journal on the following question:

- How is the pressure to succeed leading some teens—or even you—to sacrifice character?

What Do You Really Crave?

Take :05 Examine

How did I live out last week's Gospel message? What was tough? What was rewarding?

Take :05 Read

At that time Jesus was led by the Spirit into the desert to be tempted by the devil. He fasted for forty days and forty nights, and afterwards he was hungry. The tempter approached and said to him, "If you are the Son of God, command that these stones become loaves of bread." He said in reply, "It is written:

One does not live on bread alone,
> but on every word that comes forth
> from the mouth of God."

Then the devil took him to the holy city, and made him stand on the parapet of the temple, and said to him, "If you are the Son of God, throw yourself down. For it is written:

He will command his angels concerning you
> and with their hands they will support you,
lest you dash your foot against a stone."

Jesus answered him, "Again it is written,

You shall not put the Lord, your God, to the test."

Then the devil took him up to a very high mountain, and showed him all the kingdoms of the world in their magnificence, and he said to him, "All these I shall give to you, if you will prostrate yourself and worship me." At this, Jesus said to him, "Get away, Satan! It is written:

The Lord, your God, shall you worship
> and him alone shall you serve."

Then the devil left him and, behold, angels came and ministered to him.

I admire the way Muslims fast.

During their holy month of Ramadan, in the fall, Muslims abstain each day from all food and drink from sunrise to sunset. My Muslim friend Zafer once told me his hunger helps him focus on what he really craves—union with God.

This week's Gospel talks about Jesus' forty-day fast. When the devil tempts him with food, Jesus replies that "one does not live on bread alone, / but on every word that comes forth from the mouth of God." Like my friend Zafer's fast, Jesus' fast focused him on his deepest hunger—union with God.

What do you crave? Our culture creates a lot of hungers. Sometimes it might seem like we can't live without that special TV show or those shoes or that soft drink. Our consumer culture can create cravings that cause some people to choose selfishness over even friends or family. That's why fasting can be a really good thing for people. When we give up something we crave—anything from a TV show to a favorite food—we realize that we can live without it.

Why not try a strict fast this Lent? Give up something you'll really miss, like a meal each week, all drinks but water, or a favorite TV show. When the hunger comes, think instead about God and God's promises. Then ask yourself, "What do I really crave?"

Take :10 Reflect

If a word or phrase from the Gospel grabs your heart, sit quietly for several minutes, repeating it to yourself and asking God to show you how it applies to your life. Or, reflect and possibly journal on the following question:

- What can you give up for Lent that will cause you to remember your need for God?

Go Up the Mountain

Take :05 Examine

How did I live out last week's Gospel message? What was tough? What was rewarding?

Take :05 Read

Jesus took Peter, James, and John his brother, and led them up a high mountain by themselves. And he was transfigured before them; his face shone like the sun and his clothes became white as light. And behold, Moses and Elijah appeared to them, conversing with him. Then Peter said to Jesus in reply, "Lord, it is good that we are here. If you wish, I will make three tents here, one for you, one for Moses, and one for Elijah." While he was still speaking, behold, a bright cloud cast a shadow over them, then from the cloud came a voice that said, "This is my beloved Son, with whom I am well pleased; listen to him." When the disciples heard this, they fell prostrate and were very much afraid. But Jesus came and touched them, saying, "Rise, and do not be afraid." And when the disciples raised their eyes, they saw no one else but Jesus alone.

As they were coming down from the mountain, Jesus charged them, "Do not tell the vision to anyone until the Son of Man has been raised from the dead."

I wonder if Peter ever struggled with his faith before he died. After all he witnessed in Jesus' life, I bet he still had days when faith didn't make sense to him. If so, I bet his memories of Jesus—especially this week's Transfiguration—helped.

Matthew writes that Peter, James, and John saw clearly how Jesus was the fulfillment of God's promises to the world during a special spiritual experience with Jesus on a mountain.

I've had "transfiguration" experiences like that on retreats, during special Masses, or in private prayer. During those times it seems clear to me that Jesus is the answer to all I've ever wanted. But I still struggle with doubt sometimes, asking myself, "Is this God thing really sure? Or am I just kidding myself?" That's when the memories of my transfiguration experiences reassure me. They have gotten me through some tough times.

Have you had a transfiguration experience—a time on retreat, during Mass, or in prayer when it seemed certain that Jesus is the one for you? If so, thank God. It will help in hard times. Write that experience down. That way you can always remember it when doubts mount.

If you haven't had a transfiguration experience, ask God for one this Lent. Sign up for a retreat or extended service trip. During it ask God to give you the clarity the Apostles felt on that mountain. Or pray daily for that clarity and talk about your prayer with a Christian adult. Your transfiguration might happen slowly over time. Either way, I'm pretty sure a mountain is in your future.

Take :10 Reflect

If a word or phrase from the Gospel grabs your heart, sit quietly for several minutes, repeating it to yourself and asking God to show you how it applies to your life. Or, reflect and possibly journal on the following question:

• When have you felt most certain about your faith?

Grab Your Bucket and Go

Take :05 Examine

How did I live out last week's Gospel message? What was tough? What was rewarding?

Take :05 Read

Jesus came to a town of Samaria called Sychar, near the plot of land that Jacob had given to his son Joseph. Jacob's well was there. Jesus, tired from his journey, sat down there at the well. It was about noon.

A woman of Samaria came to draw water. Jesus said to her, "Give me a drink." His disciples had gone into the town to buy food. The Samaritan woman said to him, "How can you, a Jew, ask me, a Samaritan woman, for a drink?" . . . Jesus answered and said to her, "Everyone who drinks this water will be thirsty again; but whoever drinks the water I shall give will never thirst; the water I shall give will become in him a spring of water welling up to eternal life." . . .

Many of the Samaritans of that town began to believe in him because of the word of the woman . . . (John 4:5–9,13–14,39)

Bob admired this one classmate at school. Bob's classmate went around telling people they should live like Jesus, even though such behavior can be unpopular. Bob admired his courage to talk openly about faith.

Bob also admired his classmate for practicing what he preached. No one knows how many students became better Christians because of this guy's encouragement. But one thing is sure, he inspired Bob.

Bob's classmate is a modern-day, male version of the Samaritan woman—the star in this week's Gospel. The

Samaritan woman comes to a well looking for water but finds something that quenches her deepest thirst—Jesus Christ. She responds by telling everyone in town. She can't contain herself. And many people, the Gospel says, follow Jesus because of her.

What a courageous woman! Scholars write that her reputation with husbands probably made her an outsider. She also was Samaritan, from an ethnic group many Jews looked down on as a racially and religiously flawed.

The message for us? First, we can learn about God and faith from the people most put down. They often find Jesus quickly, because others turn their backs on those people. Second, we can take "living water" to others by talking openly about faith and the difference Jesus makes in our lives. Look around your home and school. I know you'll see people who thirst. Some thirst for meaning and think using alcohol and other drugs, having sex, or getting more stuff will quench their thirst. Your belief in Jesus might save a life. Some people thirst for friendship or compassion. Invite them to church or youth activities, where they can hear the stories of Jesus' love for us.

Like the Samaritan woman and Bob's classmate at school, you too can guide someone this Lent to a well of hope, peace, and comfort that never runs dry.

Take :10 Reflect

If a word or phrase from the Gospel grabs your heart, sit quietly for several minutes, repeating it to yourself and asking God to show you how it applies to your life. Or, reflect and possibly journal on the following question:

- When do you have good opportunities to share with others what your faith means to you and how you live it?

Time to Open Your Eyes?

Take :05 Examine

How did I live out last week's Gospel message? What was tough? What was rewarding?

Take :05 Read

As Jesus passed by he saw a man blind from birth. He spat on the ground and made clay with the saliva, and smeared the clay on his eyes, and said to him, "Go wash in the Pool of Siloam"— which means Sent—. So he went and washed, and came back able to see. . . .

They brought the one who was once blind to the Pharisees. Now Jesus had made clay and opened his eyes on a sabbath. So then the Pharisees also asked him how he was able to see. He said to them, "He put clay on my eyes, and I washed, and now I can see." So some of the Pharisees said, "This man is not from God, because he does not keep the sabbath." But others said, "How can a sinful man do such signs?" And there was a division among them. So they said to the blind man again, "What do you have to say about him, since he opened your eyes?" He said, "He is a prophet."

They answered and said to him, "You were born totally in sin, and are you trying to teach us?" Then they threw him out. (John 9:1,6–7,13–17,34)

I know a Christian who regularly talks to teens about how, as a young man, he abused drugs and used women. His pleasure-seeking lifestyle hurt people. He was lucky, he often tells teens, that he didn't end up dead, in jail, or a father at a young age.

The saddest thing about his talk, however, is his belief that too many teens pay no attention. He fears that, caught up in the same lifestyle and confident that they can avoid bad consequences, many teens just tune him out.

Talk about blindness!

In this week's Gospel, people refuse to learn from a miracle. Jesus heals a blind man. But people focus more on trying to discredit the miracle, the man healed, or Jesus. Ironically, the formerly blind man receives not only his sight but also the ability to see the importance of following Jesus, while the people with sight are totally blind to this.

Avoid that spiritual blindness at all costs. It is easy to stubbornly defend bad choices or a dangerous lifestyle. It can be hard to admit mistakes or to consider radically changing our habits. But God often guides us away from sinful habits that can hurt us and others. He puts people in our lives who've made similar mistakes. Listen to those people, especially when they talk about how Jesus has helped them change course.

Open your mind and eyes this Lent. Look closely at the lives of people who've counseled you to break certain habits and start new ones. You just might realize that God is trying to cure your own blindness.

Take :10 Reflect

If a word or phrase from the Gospel grabs your heart, sit quietly for several minutes, repeating it to yourself and asking God to show you how it applies to your life. Or, reflect and possibly journal on the following question:

- Have you ever stubbornly refused to follow advice, even though down deep you knew you needed to?

Where Do You Need New Life?

Take :05 Examine

How did I live out last week's Gospel message? What was tough? What was rewarding?

Take :05 Read

When Jesus arrived, he found that Lazarus had already been in the tomb for four days. When Martha heard that Jesus was coming, she went to meet him; but Mary sat at home. Martha said to Jesus, "Lord, if you had been here, my brother would not have died. But even now I know that whatever you ask of God, God will give you." Jesus said to her, "Your brother will rise."

So Jesus, perturbed again, came to the tomb. It was a cave, and a stone lay across it. Jesus said, "Take away the stone." Martha, the dead man's sister, said to him, "Lord, by now there will be a stench; he has been dead for four days." Jesus said to her, "Did I not tell you that if you believe you will see the glory of God?" So they took away the stone. And Jesus raised his eyes and said, "Father, I thank you for hearing me. I know that you always hear me; but because of the crowd here I have said this, that they may believe that you sent me." And when he had said this, he cried out in a loud voice, "Lazarus, come out!" The dead man came out, tied hand and foot with burial bands, and his face was wrapped in a cloth. So Jesus said to them, "Untie him and let him go."

Now many of the Jews who had come to Mary and seen what he had done began to believe in him. (John 11:17,20–23,38–45)

Death is frightening.

I remember how graveyards scared me as a kid. I would never walk through them at night.

Physical death isn't the only thing that frightens people. It's hard to face a relationship that is dying and work to revive it. It can also be hard not to give up when hopes die after a personal failure.

That's why we need to bring Jesus to our personal tombs, just like the sisters of Lazarus did. Martha and Mary knew Jesus could restore their dead brother to health. So, in the midst of their pain, they cried out for Jesus.

Jesus is our friend too. He weeps with us when we hurt. Just as he raised Lazarus, he can breathe life into our broken relationships and shattered hopes. So call out to him. Talk prayerfully with Jesus about problems you face with friends or family or when your life seems to hit a dead end. He will guide you out of the tomb. You might also want to seek out an adult Christian for help. Remember, Mary and Martha needed friends to bring Jesus to them. Other Christians can do that for you by lending an ear to listen or a shoulder to lean on.

Take a look this Lent at what seems dead or hopeless in your life. Remember, Jesus wants to bring you new life.

Take :10 Reflect

If a word or phrase from the Gospel grabs your heart, sit quietly for several minutes, repeating it to yourself and asking God to show you how it applies to your life. Or, reflect and possibly journal on the following question:

- What relationships or hopes seem dead in your life right now?

Palm Sunday (The Passion)
Matthew 21:1–11
At the Mass: Matthew 26:14—27:66 or 27:11–54

Face Your Tough Choices

How did I live out last week's Gospel message? What was tough? What was rewarding?

When Jesus and the disciples drew near Jerusalem and came to Bethphage on the Mount of Olives, Jesus sent two disciples, saying to them, "Go into the village opposite you, and immediately you will find an ass tethered, and a colt with her. Untie them and bring them here to me. And if anyone should say anything to you, reply, 'The master has need of them.' Then he will send them at once." . . . The disciples went and did as Jesus had ordered them. They brought the ass and the colt and laid their cloaks over them, and he sat upon them. The very large crowd spread their cloaks on the road, while others cut branches from the trees and strewed them on the road. The crowds preceding him and those following kept crying out and saying:

"Hosanna to the Son of David;

blessed is he who comes in the name of the Lord;
hosanna in the highest."

And when he entered Jerusalem the whole city was shaken and asked, "Who is this?" And the crowds replied, "This is Jesus the prophet, from Nazareth in Galilee." (Matthew 21:1–3,6–11)

One day a few years back, during a trip to Israel, I sat on the Mount of Olives, looking across the valley at Jerusalem, wondering what Jesus thought on that Palm Sunday, two thousand years ago, as he sat on the Mount of Olives.

He must have known that although many people would cheer him when he entered the city, the authorities would eventually arrest him. He must have known that death waited for him across that valley. And yet, he also must have known that he couldn't live with integrity without proclaiming his message in Jerusalem, the home of religious and political leaders who had corrupted God's message of hope and peace.

Regardless, the Gospels tell us that one day, he decided to cross that valley and enter Jerusalem. You know the rest of the story.

How about you? What decisions face you that call for sacrifice and courage? Do you have friends whose destructive behavior you should challenge? Are there people at school you should stick up for? Are there broken relationships you're afraid to repair?

Holy Week is the time to face those decisions. Watch Holy Thursday as Jesus shows you how to drop your pride and put others first. Don't miss Good Friday, where he courageously suffers and dies for what he believes. Celebrate Holy Saturday and Easter Sunday, where his Resurrection provides proof that death, violence, and fear have no ultimate power.

Pray about your hard decisions as you watch Jesus make his. You'll find him walking beside you, offering the courage and wisdom you need.

Take :10 Reflect

If a word or phrase from the Gospel grabs your heart, sit quietly for several minutes, repeating it to yourself and asking God to show you how it applies to your life. Or, reflect and possibly journal on the following question:

- What decisions face you now that call for courage?

See and Believe

Take :05   Examine

How did I live out last week's Gospel message? What was tough? What was rewarding?

Take :05   Read

On the first day of the week, Mary of Magdala came to the tomb early in the morning, while it was still dark, and saw the stone removed from the tomb. So she ran and went to Simon Peter and to the other disciple whom Jesus loved, and told them, "They have taken the Lord from the tomb, and we don't know where they put him." So Peter and the other disciple went out and came to the tomb. They both ran, but the other disciple ran faster than Peter and arrived at the tomb first; he bent down and saw the burial cloths there, but did not go in. When Simon Peter arrived after him, he went into the tomb and saw the burial cloths there, and the cloth that had covered his head, not with the burial cloths but rolled up in a separate place. Then the other disciple also went in, the one who had arrived at the tomb first, and he saw and believed. For they did not yet understand the Scripture that he had to rise from the dead.

James struggled with heroin addiction for more than ten years. His habit had left him homeless and alone. One day his doctor told him he would die within months if he kept using.

Remembering his Catholic childhood, he started going back to Mass and praying. Soon he realized that God could save him from dying a lonely junkie.

I met James soon after I joined his parish. By that time he had changed from a man craving daily heroin fixes to a man craving daily Mass. Once a man who worried only about finding money for his drugs, James now asks regularly how he can help others in the parish.

I can assure you, James believes Jesus rose from the dead.

Today we celebrate God's victory over death. The Resurrection proves that nothing can keep us from following Jesus if we call out for God's strength. We can stand up for what's right, though others may attack us. A life of sacrifice for others is possible and meaningful, though society says otherwise. Peace and freedom can be ours even though we might feel controlled by pain, fear, or bad habits.

This Easter, be like the disciple who entered the tomb and "saw and believed." See how God's power has raised others. Talk to other Christians about how God has freed them from personal problems or strengthened them to do the right thing. Where do you need strength or a new start? Do you feel trapped in a bad habit? Where do you need courage to stand for what is right or fix a broken relationship? Ask God for help. Your "resurrection" might not happen instantly. But through daily prayer and help from other Christians, someday you'll realize, just like my friend James, that you've found new life, hope, and strength.

Take :10 Reflect

If a word or phrase from the Gospel grabs your heart, sit quietly for several minutes, repeating it to yourself and asking God to show you how it applies to your life. Or, reflect and possibly journal on the following question:

- Where do you need the hope, peace, and freedom of the Resurrection in your life right now?

It's Okay to Be like Thomas

Take :05 Examine

How did I live out last week's Gospel message? What was tough? What was rewarding?

Take :05 Read

On the evening of that first day of the week, when the doors were locked, where the disciples were, for fear of the Jews, Jesus came and stood in their midst and said to them, "Peace be with you." . . .

Thomas, called Didymus, one of the Twelve, was not with them when Jesus came. So the other disciples said to him, "We have seen the Lord." But he said to them, "Unless I see the mark of the nails in his hands and put my finger into the nailmarks and put my hand into his side, I will not believe."

Now a week later his disciples were again inside and Thomas was with them. Jesus came, although the doors were locked, and stood in their midst and said, "Peace be with you." Then he said to Thomas, "Put your finger here and see my hands, and bring your hand and put it into my side, and do not be unbelieving, but believe." Thomas answered and said to him, "My Lord and my God!" Jesus said to him, "Have you come to believe because you have seen me? Blessed are those who have not seen and have believed."

Now, Jesus did many other signs in the presence of his disciples that are not written in this book. But these are written that you may come to believe that Jesus is the Christ, the Son of God, and that through this belief you may have life in his name. (John 20:19,24–31)

Thomas gets a bad rap.

This guy hears a wild story. Jesus is alive again? C'mon. That's nuts. That response from Thomas seems pretty normal to me.

And doubting your own faith is also pretty normal. Many teens start doubting their faith as they get older. They ask whether all the stories they've heard about God could really be true. You know why? Their brains change.

As you grow, your brain develops. You start thinking in new ways. You start asking more questions about life. You start challenging some things people tell you.

Don't worry if this happens. It's a normal part of growing as a disciple. But don't let this separate you from Jesus. Let it bring you closer.

Do the following when you doubt: Read more about our Catholic faith. Answer your questions. Compare Catholic beliefs with the beliefs of other faiths. Keep looking for examples of how Catholics make a difference in the world. Read about some of our past Catholic heroes. Sit with older Christians who seem devoted to God and ask them why they have that devotion. Keep praying and attending Mass. Ask God to help you sort out your doubts. Reflect on the Christian choices you make and ask yourself, "What do the results of these choices teach me about myself and the Gospel?"

Whatever you do, just don't walk away. Remember what happened when Thomas stuck around.

Take :10 Reflect

If a word or phrase from the Gospel grabs your heart, sit quietly for several minutes, repeating it to yourself and asking God to show you how it applies to your life. Or, reflect and possibly journal on the following question:

- Whom can you talk to or what can you read when you have doubts about the Gospel?

Plug into Mass

Take :05 Examine

How did I live out last week's Gospel message? What was tough? What was rewarding?

Take :05 Read

(Because of the reading's length, I can't include much here. Please read the whole passage. It is a classic.)

That very day, the first day of the week, two of Jesus' disciples were going to a village seven miles from Jerusalem called Emmaus, and they were conversing about all the things that had occurred. And it happened that while they were conversing and debating, Jesus himself drew near and walked with them, but their eyes were prevented from recognizing him. . . . And it happened that, while he was with them at table, he took bread, said the blessing, broke it, and gave it to them. With that their eyes were opened and they recognized him, but he vanished from their sight. Then they said to each other, "Were not our hearts burning within us while he spoke to us on the way and opened the Scriptures to us?" (Luke 24:13–16,30–32)

Mass is so boring.

I hear it often from teens. Many have stopped going. It saddens me, because I think they don't know what they are missing.

The Mass was critical—though it seems to have been less formal—for early Christians. They gathered on the first day of the week, told stories about Jesus, shared their hopes and fears, prayed for each other, and then shared a meal with bread and wine. Those gatherings helped them remember that Jesus was still with them. The Mass also gave them strength to live faithfully in a hostile world.

Luke tells the story in this week's Gospel in a way that shows the importance of those gatherings. The story tells about disciples' flight from Jerusalem after the Crucifixion. They talk with a stranger about the Scriptures and life. They share a meal with him, finally discovering that the stranger is Jesus. They then head back to Jerusalem filled with hope. That's the process the first Christians followed on the Sabbath—the Scriptures, reflection, bread and wine, heading back to the world in hope.

Our Mass follows the same flow today. It can also fill you with the hope of the Resurrection if you plug in. Listen closely to the readings. Compare the homily to your own reflections. Discuss the homily afterward with family or friends. During the intercessions, think about your troubles and the troubles in our world. When the Eucharistic prayer recalls how Jesus offered his body and blood to the world, quietly ask him for strength to offer yourself to make the world better. When the priest proclaims the end of the Mass, commit yourself to leaving as a disciple ready to stand for what's right.

The more you do all of that, the more you, like the disciples in the Gospel, will see Jesus is right there with you.

Take :10 Reflect

If a word or phrase from the Gospel grabs your heart, sit quietly for several minutes, repeating it to yourself and asking God to show you how it applies to your life. Or, reflect and possibly journal on the following question:

- What could you do to take more away from the Mass?

Gates Aren't All Bad

Take :05 Examine

How did I live out last week's Gospel message? What was tough? What was rewarding?

Take :05 Read

Jesus said: "Amen, amen, I say to you, whoever does not enter a sheepfold through the gate but climbs over elsewhere is a thief and a robber. But whoever enters through the gate is the shepherd of the sheep. The gatekeeper opens it for him, and the sheep hear his voice, as the shepherd calls his own sheep by name and leads them out. When he has driven out all his own, he walks ahead of them, and the sheep follow him, because they recognize his voice. But they will not follow a stranger; they will run away from him, because they do not recognize the voice of strangers." Although Jesus used this figure of speech, the Pharisees did not realize what he was trying to tell them.

So Jesus said again, "Amen, amen, I say to you, I am the gate for the sheep. All who came before me are thieves and robbers, but the sheep did not listen to them. I am the gate. Whoever enters through me will be saved, and will come in and go out and find pasture. A thief comes only to steal and slaughter and destroy; I came so that they might have life and have it more abundantly."

I remember a teen couple who were on a youth ministry camping trip. They asked if they could sleep together in a tent by the fire. "You can trust us," they promised. "We don't want to have sex until we're married."

I believed them, but I still made them sleep in separate tents—because a lot of teens make that commitment but aren't able to keep it in the heat of the moment. Those two were angry, but I'm still happy I enforced the rule.

Rules can be frustrating, but they often serve a good purpose. This week Jesus compares himself to the gate that closes the sheep's pen and keeps trouble out of their lives. Scripture scholars say that shepherds in Jesus' time actually became gates at night by sleeping across the opening to the pens.

As a teen you face a lot of rules—gates that seem to pen you in. Some come from parents, others from our Church. But the goal is to keep you from problems you might not expect.

For example, rules against sex before marriage help prevent broken hearts and unwanted pregnancies—which often lead to abortions or teen mothers raising children alone and in poverty. Rules about Mass attendance help keep teens connected to God and to the community that can help them when they face tough times.

This week, if you face a frustrating rule, ask for the reason behind it. I bet behind it, you'll find someone who loves you and who, like Jesus, wants to keep trouble out of your life.

Take :10 Reflect

If a word or phrase from the Gospel grabs your heart, sit quietly for several minutes, repeating it to yourself and asking God to show you how it applies to your life. Or, reflect and possibly journal on the following questions:

- What rules frustrate you the most? What might be the reasons behind those rules?

Be a Miracle Worker

Take :05 Examine

How did I live out last week's Gospel message? What was tough? What was rewarding?

Take :05 Read

Jesus said to his disciples: "Do not let your hearts be troubled. You have faith in God; have faith also in me." . . . "I am the way and the truth and the life. No one comes to the Father except through me. If you know me, then you will also know my Father. From now on you do know him and have seen him." Philip said to him, "Master, show us the Father, and that will be enough for us." Jesus said to him, "Have I been with you for so long a time and you still do not know me, Philip? Whoever has seen me has seen the Father. How can you say, 'Show us the Father'? Do you not believe that I am in the Father and the Father is in me? The words that I speak to you I do not speak on my own. The Father who dwells in me is doing his works. Believe me that I am in the Father and the Father is in me, or else, believe because of the works themselves. Amen, amen, I say to you, whoever believes in me will do the works that I do, and will do greater ones than these, because I am going to the Father." (John 14:1,6–12)

Fr. Louis Querbes believed in young people.

He was a nineteenth-century French priest who decided to help poor rural kids who couldn't afford school—which condemned them to ignorance and poverty. How did Father Querbes respond? He formed an order of brothers and priests to teach them and named the order after his town's patron, Saint Viator. Today, Viatorian brothers and priests serve young people in more than fifteen countries. I am amazed when I think about the tens of thousands of young people whose lives have improved through many generations because Father Querbes believed in Jesus and acted.

What a miracle!

Father Querbes is important to me because I'm a Viatorian—and because Viatorians helped me in high school, when I was lonely and full of self-doubt.

Jesus' followers will do greater works than he did, according to this week's Gospel. Sound impossible?

It's not. Jesus is right. Through the ages Christians have helped billions of people in his name. Ever needed a hospital? Christians started many ancient and modern hospitals. Want to go to college? Christians were key in starting the first universities in Europe and the Americas. Want to help the poor? Christian agencies help millions each day. Connect with one.

Although some people through the ages have done horrible things in Jesus' name, the good Jesus' followers have done far outweighs that. Take Jesus up on his words this week. Live the Gospel. Act for others. Like the founder of my religious order, you'll be amazed at the miracles God works through you.

Take :10 Reflect

If a word or phrase from the Gospel grabs your heart, sit quietly for several minutes, repeating it to yourself and asking God to show you how it applies to your life. Or, reflect and possibly journal on the following question:

- What good have you seen God work through your life or the life or other Christians?

You Have a Defender

Take :05 Examine

How did I live out last week's Gospel message? What was tough? What was rewarding?

Take :05 Read

Jesus said to his disciples: "If you love me, you will keep my commandments. And I will ask the Father, and he will give you another Advocate to be with you always, the Spirit of truth, whom the world cannot accept, because it neither sees nor knows him. But you know him, because he remains with you, and will be in you. I will not leave you orphans; I will come to you. In a little while the world will no longer see me, but you will see me, because I live and you will live. On that day you will realize that I am in my Father and you are in me and I in you. Whoever has my commandments and observes them is the one who loves me. And whoever loves me will be loved by my Father, and I will love him and reveal myself to him."

A catechist once told me about a teen in her youth group whose family struggled with alcohol abuse. She lived through drunken arguments each weekend.

Unfortunately, her story is common. Alcoholism, drug abuse, and domestic violence plague thousands of homes. In fact, some teens in these homes even feel orphaned, alone, and unable to trust any family member, regardless of how many people live with them.

You might be one of those teens. Or someone you know might suffer this way. But John, this week's Gospel writer, reassures us that Jesus hasn't left us orphans. Jesus' Spirit lives with us as an advocate, a defender who stands by and for us. That was important news for the early Christians who heard stories about Jesus but never knew him. John's passage this week reassured them that Jesus' power would still help them face trials.

Reread John's advice. Observe Jesus' commandments, and you'll realize Jesus also will defend you. If you ever feel orphaned, you'll find Jesus with you when you do what he did: pray, read the Scriptures, worship with others, and reach out to faith-filled people (adults and teens) for help. You'll also find him close by and reassuring you when you serve and sacrifice for other people, as he did. The more you do that, the more you'll build self-confidence that will help you weather tough times at home.

If you don't face problems at home, remember that we, Christ's Body today, should stand with others who feel orphaned by problems at home. How can you reach out to another teen who lives in a pain-filled home?

It's still Easter, during which we celebrate how God brings hope and peace from suffering. Live Jesus' commandments, and you'll see victory in homes where pain seems overwhelming.

Take :10 Reflect

If a word or phrase from the Gospel grabs your heart, sit quietly for several minutes, repeating it to yourself and asking God to show you how it applies to your life. Or, reflect and possibly journal on the following questions:

- How can you help a friend with problems at home? How can living Jesus' commandments help you with your problems at home?

Living for Honors Versus Living Honorably

Take :05 Examine

How did I live out last week's Gospel message? What was tough? What was rewarding?

Take :05 Read

Jesus raised his eyes to heaven and said, "Father, the hour has come. Give glory to your son, so that your son may glorify you, just as you gave him authority over all people, so that your son may give eternal life to all you gave him. Now this is eternal life, that they should know you, the only true God, and the one whom you sent, Jesus Christ. I glorified you on earth by accomplishing the work that you gave me to do. Now glorify me, Father, with you, with the glory that I had with you before the world began." (John 17:1–5)

I remember the best student speech I ever heard. Carlos was number one in his senior class when he addressed his classmates at graduation. His speech didn't focus on strategies for career success. Rather, he challenged his peers to live their Catholic education by building a better world and living for others.

Here was a highly honored young man for whom living honorably was more important than chasing honors.

In this week's Gospel, Jesus asks God to give him glory. According to a Scripture scholar, *glory* really means "honor." In other words, Jesus' prayer asks God to recognize and show others that his lifestyle—a life of service, compassion, and prayer—is the most honorable way to live. And honor was important in Jesus' time. People fought and killed to protect their honor and avoid shame. But Jesus turned the notion of honor upside down. For him, honor meant living for God and others, not for status, power, or wealth.

Don't you think that today our society still gets confused over the real meaning of honor? Too many people, young and old, strive for honors but do so dishonorably. They lie on their taxes or term papers. They attack others if they think they've been insulted. They climb the ladder of success at school or work, even if that means using the people they work or study with. Meanwhile, others are rarely honored for truly honorable works—the hours they spend helping in nursing homes, leading retreats, or befriending lonely people.

In the end don't we all want people to look at our lives and, like Jesus, thank God that we lived honorably? In the end won't honorable living—honesty, compassion, and sacrifice for others—make our lives truly worthwhile?

Take time this last week of Easter to check out your definition of *honor*. And remember Jesus' promise: an honorable life isn't the easiest or most glamorous, but it's a life that changes the world and gives glory to God.

Take :10 Reflect

If a word or phrase from the Gospel grabs your heart, sit quietly for several minutes, repeating it to yourself and asking God to show you how it applies to your life. Or, reflect and possibly journal on the following question:

* Who inspires you by the honorable way he or she lives?

Don't Bundle Up Against This Wind

Take :05 Examine

How did I live out last week's Gospel message? What was tough? What was rewarding?

Take :05 Read

On the evening of that first day of the week, when the doors were locked, where the disciples were, for fear of the Jews, Jesus came and stood in their midst and said to them, "Peace be with you." When he had said this, he showed them his hands and his side. The disciples rejoiced when they saw the Lord. Jesus said to them again, "Peace be with you. As the Father has sent me, so I send you." And when he had said this, he breathed on them and said to them, "Receive the Holy Spirit. Whose sins you forgive are forgiven them, and whose sins you retain are retained."

Boy, I love a cool breeze on a hot and humid day. But boy, I hate those biting winds that cut right through me in winter.

That's the wind for you. Sometimes it refreshes you. Sometimes it shakes you up.

Just like the Holy Spirit.

This week we celebrate Pentecost, the day when the first Apostles realized that God's Spirit was with them. The Gospel tells this story by recalling how Jesus gave his Apostles the Holy Spirit with a breath. Scripture scholars say that our ancestors described the Spirit of God as a breath or breeze because the wind was one of the most powerful and mysterious forces they witnessed. Just like God's Spirit, it could tear down or refresh, and they could never control it.

Although we can't control the Holy Spirit, we can still take advantage of its power. It can refresh us when fear, uncertainties, or broken relationships wear us out. It shakes us up when we've done something wrong. It can give us power to stand for justice by doing things like serving the poor, stopping gossip, and marching for peace. It can lead us on adventures.

Here's an example. Sue is a friend of mine who never dreamed of working in ministry when she was in college. One day her former youth minister dragged her to a conference on youth ministry. She went reluctantly. But some things the speaker said stuck with her, and soon she felt something pushing her in a new direction. Though she resisted at first, she eventually gave in and now works as a parish youth minister, helping kids connect with the Spirit that led her to them and has made her life so exciting.

How do you respond to this sacred wind? The Holy Spirit enters your life through prayer, the Scriptures, the sacraments, and people who care for you. You can feel its breeze when your conscience stirs, your dreams soar, or your heart aches for someone in pain. Be willing to let the Spirit take you where God wants, as the Apostles did. Don't bundle up against it. Let it carry you on an adventure.

Take :10 Reflect

If a word or phrase from the Gospel grabs your heart, sit quietly for several minutes, repeating it to yourself and asking God to show you how it applies to your life. Or, reflect and possibly journal on the following question:

- When have you felt the Spirit tug at your conscience or move you to help others?

Trinity Sunday
John 3:16–18

Saved Through Relationships

How did I live out last week's Gospel message? What was tough? What was rewarding?

God so loved the world that he gave his only Son, so that everyone who believes in him might not perish but might have eternal life. For God did not send his Son into the world to condemn the world, but that the world might be saved through him. Whoever believes in him will not be condemned, but whoever does not believe has already been condemned, because he has not believed in the name of the only Son of God.

When I first joined my religious order, the Viatorians, I was a different person. Although I wanted to serve God, I had a lot of character flaws. I was very judgmental, selfish, and insensitive.

Thank God for my Viatorian brothers. Through them Jesus has saved me from those flaws. Over the years my brothers have challenged me and forgiven me, inspired me to change, and been patient when I couldn't. I'm still far from perfect, but I'm a much better Christian now because of my relationships with them.

And that leads us to the Trinity and this week's Gospel. First, the Trinity. The Church believes that God's very self is a relationship—among Father, Son, and Holy Spirit. And that relationship pours love into the world. Aren't we similar? Just like God, relationships are central to our nature. Our friendships build us up or tear us down. They help us fulfill our dreams or they get in the way.

That brings us to this week's Gospel. The Holy Trinity, this God of relationships, seeks to save the world, not condemn it. Do your relationships do the same thing? Do your friends challenge you to live a holier life? Do you hang out with people who inspire you to goodness and compassion? Is the world around you and your friends a better place when you all get together?

I remember one young man from a parish I once served. For quite some time, he hung out with people who skipped school and smoked pot. That became his lifestyle. After I met him, he became involved in our parish youth ministry. He started hanging out more with people who worked to improve themselves and their world through prayer, hard work at school, and service retreats. Those relationships helped change him into a retreat leader—which then helped change the world around him.

This week remember that the Holy Trinity's relationship changes the world. Then think about your relationships with friends. Do some comparing. Hopefully, you'll see that you're a lot more like the Trinity than you think.

Take :10 Reflect

If a word or phrase from the Gospel grabs your heart, sit quietly for several minutes, repeating it to yourself and asking God to show you how it applies to your life. Or, reflect and possibly journal on the following questions:

- How do your friends' relationships with you help them follow Jesus? Do those relationships ever hurt their ability to follow Jesus?

Christ's Really Here—Are You?

Take :05 Examine

How did I live out last week's Gospel message? What was tough? What was rewarding?

Take :05 Read

Jesus said to the Jewish crowds:"I am the living bread that came down from heaven; whoever eats this bread will live forever; and the bread that I will give is my flesh for the life of the world."

The Jews quarreled among themselves, saying, "How can this man give us his flesh to eat?" Jesus said to them, "Amen, amen, I say to you, unless you eat the flesh of the Son of Man and drink his blood, you do not have life within you. Whoever eats my flesh and drinks my blood has eternal life, and I will raise him on the last day." (John 6:51–54)

I know a young man who went through times so tough that he entered a rehabilitation program for people suffering depression. He took only a few things with him. One was a picture of him with his closest friends. I believe he took that because it reminded him how much they cared, and those memories gave him strength and comfort during his tough times.

Don't we all have pictures or letters we keep close for lonely nights or painful days? We find them when we need a reminder that people really do care. I don't know about you, but the people I love seem really present when I see them in a picture or read letters they wrote to me.

If that makes sense to you, then you are on your way to understanding Christ's real presence in the Eucharist. Early Christians scared some people because they talked about eating someone's body and blood. Obviously that's not what Christians do. But Christ is fully present in the forms of bread and wine, even though you cannot physically observe it.

Remembering a close friend who isn't physically present can remind you that you are loved and cared for. Your friend's presence can still be very real at those times. How much more can Jesus Christ—who is truly present in the Eucharist—offer us comfort, strength, and challenge when we eat and drink at the Eucharistic table.

Here's something else to think about. This week don't ask whether Christ is really present during the Mass. Ask yourself whether *you* are really present. Let's say you call a friend on the phone for help. He or she can be really present as a good listener and adviser. But if you aren't really present—if you don't pay attention or open your mind—then you're likely to miss the support your friend is offering. The same is true during the Eucharist. Focus in the coming weeks on being really present during Mass. Greet the people sitting next to you. Listen and respond to the prayers and readings. Sing the songs. As you receive the body and blood, pray for strength and guidance in problems you face. I guarantee you'll meet a great friend there just waiting for you.

Take :10 Reflect

If a word or phrase from the Gospel grabs your heart, sit quietly for several minutes, repeating it to yourself and asking God to show you how it applies to your life. Or, reflect and possibly journal on the following question:

- When have you found strength, hope, comfort, or peace during a Mass?

Time to Build

Take :05 Examine

How did I live out last week's Gospel message? What was tough? What was rewarding?

Take :05 Read

Jesus said to his disciples: "Not everyone who says to me, 'Lord, Lord,' will enter the kingdom of heaven, but only the one who does the will of my Father in heaven. Many will say to me on that day, 'Lord, Lord, did we not prophesy in your name? Did we not drive out demons in your name? Did we not do mighty deeds in your name?' Then I will declare to them solemnly, 'I never knew you. Depart from me, you evildoers.'

"Everyone who listens to these words of mine and acts on them will be like a wise man who built his house on rock. The rain fell, the floods came, and the winds blew and buffeted the house. But it did not collapse; it had been set solidly on rock. And everyone who listens to these words of mine but does not act on them will be like a fool who built his house on sand. The rain fell, the floods came, and the winds blew and buffeted the house. And it collapsed and was completely ruined."

Never forget Christopher Reeve.

He played Superman in movies. He was wealthy, popular, attractive, and fit. Then one day he broke his neck riding a horse, and he could no longer use his arms or legs.

But that didn't ruin him. In fact, his life seemed to take on new meaning as he worked endlessly for a cure to paralysis. This man, who could move only a few muscles, changed the lives of millions by raising money to fight paralysis.

Ironically, he became a real "superman" after his body broke down.

This week Jesus talks about life's harsh realities. Don't count on your popularity, academic success, or physical talents to make your life meaningful. As Christopher Reeve discovered, it all can change in an instant. Life is full of storms. You will fail. You will experience loneliness. You will get older. Your body will break down.

Then where will you turn? Thanks to God we have a rock for security during those storms. He is Jesus, the Christ. Because of him we can find a meaningful life regardless of the storms that hit us—just as Christopher Reeve did. That's good news, but it's also a warning. As a teen you set priorities and develop habits for living. Build your house on a rock by developing Christian habits.

Pray daily. Learn to lengthen your daily prayer time. Join a Christian group, where people know you and are there for you in tough times. Regularly serve those who suffer. It will remind you of how much you can offer regardless of your success, beauty, wealth, or popularity. Learn to forgive and apologize. That will build you a circle of faithful friends.

Build your solid foundation now. The storms will come.

Take :10 Reflect

If a word or phrase from the Gospel grabs your heart, sit quietly for several minutes, repeating it to yourself and asking God to show you how it applies to your life. Or, reflect and possibly journal on the following question:

- What are the foundations—the basic beliefs, values, and habits—that you are building in your life?

Hey, You Sinner. Forgetting Something?

Take :05 Examine

How did I live out last week's Gospel message? What was tough? What was rewarding?

Take :05 Read

As Jesus passed on from there, he saw a man named Matthew sitting at the customs post. He said to him, "Follow me." And he got up and followed him. While he was at table in his house, many tax collectors and sinners came and sat with Jesus and his disciples. The Pharisees saw this and said to his disciples, "Why does your teacher eat with tax collectors and sinners?" He heard this and said, "Those who are well do not need a physician, but the sick do. Go and learn the meaning of the words, 'I desire mercy, not sacrifice.' I did not come to call the righteous but sinners."

You're a sinner.

"Oh sure," you say, "I know that." Unfortunately too many teens see only their flaws. And they think God has little use for them.

I once asked teens preparing for Confirmation if they thought they shared Christ's divine nature. They thought I was crazy. "Divine? Yeah, right," their eyes responded.

But it's true. You are created in the image of God. You have within you the Spirit of God. A goodness is within you that you can't lose—despite your worst sins. I just wish more teens realized that. It would change how they see themselves and the world.

Jesus knew that. He knew that each person carries a divine spark that can burst into a flame. In fact, he focused most of his time trying to ignite those sparks in the people who thought they had little to offer—the sinners of his time.

This week he calls Matthew. Scripture scholars say that back then, common folks often hated tax collectors. They worked for the Romans, the occupying army, and could make taxes as high as they wanted—as long as they paid a license fee to the Romans. Many people saw the tax collectors as traitors who ripped off their own people. What good could they do?

Jesus saw things differently. He saw potential in each person. He probably knew that the divine spark in people ignites when someone believes in those people and gives them a chance to make a difference.

Jesus sees the same potential in you. That's right. So own up to your worst sins. But realize that Jesus sees goodness within you that you might miss.

Look in the mirror today. If you don't see your goodness, look harder and ask Jesus to point it out. If you're troubled by sin, seek reconciliation with a priest and anyone you've hurt. Then focus on showing your goodness to people, and you'll find it easier to avoid sins.

You are worthy. Be amazed today that God, knowing your flaws, still calls out lovingly each day, "Follow me. . . . I believe in you."

Take :10 Reflect

If a word or phrase from the Gospel grabs your heart, sit quietly for several minutes, repeating it to yourself and asking God to show you how it applies to your life. Or, reflect and possibly journal on the following question:

- How can teens always remember that their divinity outweighs their sins?

No Time to Wait

Take :05 Examine

How did I live out last week's Gospel message? What was tough? What was rewarding?

Take :05 Read

At the sight of the crowds, Jesus' heart was moved with pity for them because they were troubled and abandoned, like sheep without a shepherd. Then he said to his disciples, "The harvest is abundant but the laborers are few; so ask the master of the harvest to send out laborers for his harvest."

Then he summoned his twelve disciples and gave them authority over unclean spirits to drive them out and to cure every disease and every illness. The names of the twelve apostles are these: first, Simon called Peter, and his brother Andrew; James, the son of Zebedee, and his brother John; Philip and Bartholomew, Thomas and Matthew the tax collector; James, the son of Alphaeus, and Thaddeus; Simon from Cana, and Judas Iscariot who betrayed him.

Jesus sent out these twelve after instructing them thus, "Do not go into pagan territory or enter a Samaritan town. Go rather to the lost sheep of the house of Israel. As you go, make this proclamation: 'The kingdom of heaven is at hand.' Cure the sick, raise the dead, cleanse lepers, drive out demons. Without cost you have received; without cost you are to give."

On a retreat once, a young man in tears asked me how to improve his relationship with his terminally ill mother.

At my parish once, a mother asked me to involve her son in parish activities to keep him from falling into gang life.

There's no time to waste. People need Christ's Good News now.

That's a message from this week's Gospel. Some Scripture scholars believe Jesus thought that the world's end, and God's Reign, was right around the corner. So he urgently gathered disciples and sent them to proclaim his message throughout Israel.

Well, we know now that the world hasn't ended. God's Reign hasn't fully arrived. Nonetheless, millions of people need us to make it real for them *right now*. People in your family, school, and community face problems or injustices that worsen by the moment. Time is critical. *Right now* they need people who bring them God's message by living like Jesus.

This week, remember that. Look out for people who need your help immediately. Which people in your school, home, or community face relationships that are falling apart, loneliness that is crushing them, or economic problems that are driving them to hunger or homelessness? Keep your eyes and ears open. Live the Lord's Prayer by making the Kingdom come to them through your actions.

Take :10 Reflect

If a word or phrase from the Gospel grabs your heart, sit quietly for several minutes, repeating it to yourself and asking God to show you how it applies to your life. Or, reflect and possibly journal on the following questions:

- Where do you see people struggling with problems that need help urgently? What can you do?

Don't Let Fear Threaten Your Soul

Take :05 Examine

How did I live out last week's Gospel message? What was tough? What was rewarding?

Take :05 Read

Jesus said to the Twelve: "Fear no one. Nothing is concealed that will not be revealed, nor secret that will not be known. What I say to you in the darkness, speak in the light; what you hear whispered, proclaim on the housetops. And do not be afraid of those who kill the body but cannot kill the soul; rather, be afraid of the one who can destroy both soul and body in Gehenna. Are not two sparrows sold for a small coin? Yet not one of them falls to the ground without your Father's knowledge. Even all the hairs of your head are counted. So do not be afraid; you are worth more than many sparrows. Everyone who acknowledges me before others I will acknowledge before my heavenly Father. But who-ever denies me before others, I will deny before my heavenly Father."

I remember being afraid in high school.

I remember fearing the bullies when I was a freshman. I remember fearing rejection as I looked for friends. I remember fearing humiliation when I asked girls for a date. Sadly, I did some stupid things out of fear, some things that hurt my character.

Fear is real, but it doesn't have to control us, because God cares enough to stand by us through it all. That's the good news from this week's Gospel.

Early Christians also struggled with fear. Remember, they were Jewish and saw Jesus as the fulfillment of all Jewish hopes. That belief put them in conflict with other Jews, who eventually kicked those early Christians out of their communities. Read the Acts of the Apostles or Saint Paul's letters. You'll find some hair-raising stories about the persecutions they faced.

Nonetheless, they persevered. They believed that Jesus' teachings helped them grow closer to God. So they developed strong worship lives that soothed and strengthened their souls. They devoted themselves to helping one another. All this, they found, brought them God's strength—strength that helped them face rejection and brutality.

That strength can be yours. Call upon it. It's scary to risk your popularity, to challenge bullies, to stand against bigotry and dishonesty, and to stand up for sobriety and sexual abstinence. You are likely to face rejection and maybe even physical attack. But you build so much character when you take those risks. Those risks strengthen your soul.

Follow the examples of those early Christians. Make Mass and Christian activities important in your life. They will protect your soul and calm your fears. You will find, as Jesus says, that God watches you closely, always looking for ways to help you out.

Take :10 Reflect

If a word or phrase from the Gospel grabs your heart, sit quietly for several minutes, repeating it to yourself and asking God to show you how it applies to your life. Or, reflect and possibly journal on the following question:

• What Christian decisions cause or have caused you to fear?

Up for a Workout?

Take :05 Examine

How did I live out last week's Gospel message? What was
tough? What was rewarding?

Take :05 Read

*Jesus said to his apostles: "Whoever loves father or mother more
than me is not worthy of me, and whoever loves son or daughter
more than me is not worthy of me; and whoever does not take
up his cross and follow after me is not worthy of me. Whoever
finds his life will lose it, and whoever loses his life for my sake will
find it.*

*"Whoever receives you receives me, and whoever receives me
receives the one who sent me. Whoever receives a prophet
because he is a prophet will receive a prophet's reward, and
whoever receives a righteous man because he is a righteous
man will receive a righteous man's reward. And whoever gives
only a cup of cold water to one of these little ones to drink
because the little one is a disciple—amen, I say to you, he will
surely not lose his reward."*

I once ran with the Olympic torch.

Before each new Olympic games, runners carry the
torch from Athens, Greece, to the Olympics site. They pass
it from runner to runner for thousands of miles. I joined
the relay for about a mile when it came through Las Vegas,
where I lived at the time, though I carried the torch only
briefly.

I trained as a runner before the day the torch came
through. Nothing would be more embarrassing, I thought,

than huffing and puffing with the torch in my hand. At first I hated running, and my body seemed to hate me for doing it. But over time it got easier and easier.

Here's how this all connects to this week's Gospel. Jesus tells us that discipleship requires serious sacrifice. It costs to follow Jesus. You have to forgive, to care for your enemies, to give your time, to share your money, to do the right thing when it's not popular. Discipleship might even seem like an impossible challenge at times.

But living as a disciple is like training for a race. Little sacrifices help train you for bigger ones. Practice as a Christian builds up your strength. Give a little time regularly to others. Forgive people for little hurts. Be honest in small matters. The more you make little sacrifices, the easier it will be to make bigger ones in the future—sacrifices that might make a big difference in the world. Don't get discouraged when you seem to fail. Just keep training. And look to your loving, forgiving coach—Jesus—who wants to guide and encourage you.

Take :10 Reflect

If a word or phrase from the Gospel grabs your heart, sit quietly for several minutes, repeating it to yourself and asking God to show you how it applies to your life. Or, reflect and possibly journal on the following question:

- What little sacrifices could you make now that would help your Christian training?

All Tied Up?

Take :05 Examine

How did I live out last week's Gospel message? What was tough? What was rewarding?

Take :05 Read

At that time Jesus exclaimed: "I give praise to you, Father, Lord of heaven and earth, for although you have hidden these things from the wise and the learned you have revealed them to little ones. Yes, Father, such has been your gracious will. All things have been handed over to me by my Father. No one knows the Son except the Father, and no one knows the Father except the Son and anyone to whom the Son wishes to reveal him."

"Come to me, all you who labor and are burdened, and I will give you rest. Take my yoke upon you and learn from me, for I am meek and humble of heart; and you will find rest for yourselves. For my yoke is easy, and my burden light."

I see too many teens who put on "yokes."

Farmers put yokes on oxen to tie them to a plow. Oxen tied to yokes have no freedom. They go where the farmer commands—just like people with bad habits or addictions.

I remember a junior once telling me that he saw nothing dangerous about his very active sex life. I pray that he hasn't put on the yoke of sex addiction, which can develop when people seek out sex no matter what the risks might be.

I remember a senior who was the life of every party every weekend—mostly because he was drunk. I pray that he hasn't put on the yoke of alcoholism, which can take hold of teens quickly who make alcohol a focus of their social life.

I remember a junior I caught cheating on a test. I pray that she hasn't put on the yoke of habitual dishonesty, which destroys a person's inner character and outer reputation. It can develop quickly from little lies and "borrowed" homework.

This week Jesus invites us to take his yoke. "Let me and my teachings guide every decision you make," he pleads. "I'll lead you to peace and meaning in this life and union with God in the next one."

He's right, you know. Many years ago I took his advice. I still struggle against him, at times, even going way off course. But he always gently pulls me back. And as I've let him guide me, I've found rest (meaning, happiness, friendships) that other yokes just can't offer.

Examine your life this week. See if you are tying yourself to a yoke that could hurt you. If so, ask Jesus for help to break free. Then take on his yoke. You'll never look back with regret.

Take :10 Reflect

If a word or phrase from the Gospel grabs your heart, sit quietly for several minutes, repeating it to yourself and asking God to show you how it applies to your life. Or, reflect and possibly journal on the following question:

- Do you make any regular choices that could develop into bad habits or addictions that could hurt you or others?

Fifteenth Sunday in Ordinary Time
Matthew 13:1–23 or Matthew 13:1–9

Patience, Patience: Part 1

Take :05 Examine

How did I live out last week's Gospel message? What was tough? What was rewarding?

Take :05 Read

On that day, Jesus went out of the house and sat down by the sea. Such large crowds gathered around him that he got into a boat and sat down, and the whole crowd stood along the shore. And he spoke to them at length in parables, saying: "A sower went out to sow. And as he sowed, some seed fell on the path, and birds came and ate it up. Some fell on rocky ground, where it had little soil. It sprang up at once because the soil was not deep, and when the sun rose it was scorched, and it withered for lack of roots. Some seed fell among thorns, and the thorns grew up and choked it. But some seed fell on rich soil and produced fruit, a hundred or sixty or thirtyfold. Whoever has ears ought to hear." (Matthew 13:1–9)

"I can't believe I did *that* again!"

I've said it many times. You might have said it a few times, as well.

I know a lot of teens struggle with discouragement as they try to become better people who grow closer to God and make holier decisions. Ever get the feeling that you just aren't going to be able to do it? You're just going to keep repeating the same sins over and over? Or, you just can't kick some behavior that causes problems with friends and family?

If so, you're not alone. Welcome to the Christian community. There's some real wisdom in this week's Gospel for folks like you and me. Jesus used a lot of farming examples, because many of the people who followed him lived off the land. This week he compares the word of God to a seed that needs fertile ground to take root.

Here are some important points from that comparison. First, God seeds the world with the divine word. God's word is powerful. Like a seed, it has all it needs to grow in our lives and bear fruit that will change us and the world around us. We don't have to worry about figuring out a way to live a happy life. The word will guide us to that.

Second, we only need to make our lives fertile ground for the word. If we do, God's strength and wisdom will naturally grow in us over time. That's good news because, like a plant, the word needs time to grow in us. Don't worry about being perfect. You are going to sin. You'll back down at the wrong times. You'll hurt people at times. But if you let God's word grow in you as you grow older, you'll find yourself sinning less often, standing up for what's right more often, and making fewer mistakes that hurt people.

Say sorry when you need to. Repair relationships when you make mistakes. But be patient with yourself as you grow into a mature disciple. Keep trying. And keep your soul fertile by reading the word regularly, going to Mass, and serving those who suffer in our world.

Someday you'll be amazed at what God has planted in you.

Take :10 Reflect

If a word or phrase from the Gospel grabs your heart, sit quietly for several minutes, repeating it to yourself and asking God to show you how it applies to your life. Or, reflect and possibly journal on the following question:

- In what ways are you impatient about your growth as a Christian?

Patience, Patience: Part 2

Take :05 Examine

How did I live out last week's Gospel message? What was tough? What was rewarding?

Take :05 Read

Jesus proposed another parable to the crowds, saying: "The kingdom of heaven may be likened to a man who sowed good seed in his field. While everyone was asleep his enemy came and sowed weeds all through the wheat, and then went off. When the crop grew and bore fruit, the weeds appeared as well. The slaves of the householder came to him and said, 'Master, did you not sow good seed in your field? Where have the weeds come from?' He answered, 'An enemy has done this.' His slaves said to him, 'Do you want us to go and pull them up?' He replied, 'No, if you pull up the weeds you might uproot the wheat along with them. Let them grow together until harvest; then at harvest time I will say to the harvesters, "First collect the weeds and tie them in bundles for burning; but gather the wheat into my barn."'"
(Matthew 13:24–30)

(Take a moment to reread last week's reflection before starting this one.)

Okay, others deserve my patience too—which is hard for me to remember.

I can be brutally judgmental. I can see one bad trait in a person and think to myself, "That guy is worthless."

What a horrible thought! Especially for a Christian—and a priest. Do you ever find yourself reducing a person to that one bad habit? Do you ever struggle to see the good in people who sometimes tick you off?

Welcome to the Christian community. We fall into that way of thinking pretty darn easily. That's why this Gospel is a good read for all of us.

Notice. The farmer tells his workers not to pull up the weeds. He's afraid of damaging the good crops. "Wait until the harvest," he says. "We'll separate everything then." What patience and confidence! He's not at all nervous about the weeds destroying the good crops!

And that's the type of patience and confidence God has in people. Each of us is a combination of good crop and weeds. God sees our character flaws and sins. But he focuses much more on the good crop we are sprouting—our good traits and the positive things we do for others. If God is so patient with people's flaws, can't we be patient with the flaws in others? If God looks so hard to see our goodness, can't we look harder for the goodness in those who sometimes irritate us? If God wants to affirm us for our strengths rather than judge us for our sins, can't we go out of our way to affirm the good things we see in the people whose limits frustrate us?

Sure, we're not God. I'm reminded of that daily when I want to write someone off. Here's what I do. I pray daily for the people I judge harshly and ask God to help me see them with divine eyes. I also ask for immediate help during those moments in the day when I find myself judging. Why not join me? Let's work together to nurture the good crop that sometimes we don't see in other folks.

Take :10 Reflect

If a word or phrase from the Gospel grabs your heart, sit quietly for several minutes, repeating it to yourself and asking God to show you how it applies to your life. Or, reflect and possibly journal on the following question:

- Can you identify a good trait in one or two people with whom you don't get along?

All Really Does Mean "All"

Take :05 Examine

How did I live out last week's Gospel message? What was tough? What was rewarding?

Take :05 Read

Jesus said to his disciples: "The kingdom of heaven is like a treasure buried in a field, which a person finds and hides again, and out of joy goes and sells all that he has and buys that field. Again, the kingdom of heaven is like a merchant searching for fine pearls. When he finds a pearl of great price, he goes and sells all that he has and buys it." (Matthew 13:44–46)

A few years ago, a U.S. Olympic skater shocked the world.

After winning the gold medal, he lectured the world about its not stopping the slaughter of innocent people in a war-torn African country. He also announced that he would donate his $25,000 prize to help that country's refugees.

Wait a second, I thought! No comments about his goals? No pro-U.S.A. chant? No thanking God for his victory?

No, just a guy using his talents to make the world a better place—instead of using them only for his benefit. I don't know what religion he practiced, but it sounded like a Catholic who had just read this week's Gospel.

Too many people seem to think the Gospel is a Sunday thing. Or they think religion belongs in the classroom or the church but not in the workplace, in the cafeteria, or on the practice field.

Not so, Jesus says this week. We need to give our all to God. That doesn't necessarily mean giving away all we own.

But it does mean living the Gospel in all areas of our lives. Sure, we talk about Jesus in religion classes or youth groups. But do we treat people as Jesus would treat them in the big game or act as Jesus would act at weekend parties?

Look at your life. Does your family need some understanding? Are there kids in the lunchroom who need companionship? Does your boss have an honest employee? Do you treat sports opponents with respect? Do you ever pass on buying that CD or DVD to give money to the poor?

Mature disciples learn to give their all to the Gospel by living it in every area of life. They show others how valuable God's Reign is to them by standing for it in every group or activity. Like the Olympic skater, their actions inspire others.

Make a chart this week that breaks your life into sections like sports, family, school, weekends, and so on. In each section list how the Gospel does or should guide your actions. Honestly ask yourself whether you are a Christian in all areas of your life. Then ask Jesus for help to make any changes necessary.

To be a part of God's Reign, *all* really does mean "all." That's not easy, but as far as I'm concerned, all I want is to see God's Reign taking shape around me.

Take :10 Reflect

If a word or phrase from the Gospel grabs your heart, sit quietly for several minutes, repeating it to yourself and asking God to show you how it applies to your life. Or, reflect and possibly journal on the following question:

• In what areas of your life is it hardest to give your all to the Gospel?

You Have Enough; Share It!

Take :05 Examine

How did I live out last week's Gospel message? What was tough? What was rewarding?

Take :05 Read

When [Jesus] disembarked and saw the vast crowd, his heart was moved with pity for them, and he cured their sick. When it was evening, the disciples approached him and said, "This is a deserted place and it is already late; dismiss the crowds so that they can go to the villages and buy food for themselves." Jesus said to them, "There is no need for them to go away; give them some food yourselves." But they said to him, "Five loaves and two fish are all we have here." Then he said, "Bring them here to me," and he ordered the crowds to sit down on the grass. Taking the five loaves and the two fish, and looking up to heaven, he said the blessing, broke the loaves, and gave them to the disciples, who in turn gave them to the crowds. They all ate and were satisfied, and they picked up the fragments left over— twelve wicker baskets full. Those who ate were about five thousand men, not counting women and children. (Matthew 14:14–21)

I often see it in their eyes when I encourage teens to make the world better in Christ's name. I see a lack of confidence, a look saying, "I have nothing to give. I'm not special in that way."

I felt that way for many years as a teen. I lacked confidence and struggled with self-doubt. I thought I had very little to offer other people or the world's problems. And that didn't feel good. I know that teens who feel that way—and many do—spend a lot of time sad.

But each person is a gift from God to the world, with some talent the world needs. Sometimes it just takes a little time to discover that talent.

This week's Gospel is good for teens lacking confidence. Jesus faces a hungry crowd. The disciples don't think they can help. Things change, though, when they give their food to Jesus. It feeds thousands.

That's the lesson for us. Our cupboards are full. Each of us has "food" to offer the world, though sometimes we don't realize it. I know many teens who are shocked by the difference they make by leading youth groups, volunteering, or just listening to friends who need help.

It's only when you start reaching out to help that you'll realize how much "food" you have to offer our world, which is hungry for peace, forgiveness, and compassion. You will gain more and more confidence. I did.

List your talents. If that is hard to do, ask a friend or teacher for help. Pray for help too. Jesus sees more talent in you than you realize. Offer him your "loaves and fish" and then watch him work a miracle.

Take :10 Reflect

If a word or phrase from the Gospel grabs your heart, sit quietly for several minutes, repeating it to yourself and asking God to show you how it applies to your life. Or, reflect and possibly journal on the following question:

- How can teens who struggle with self-doubt build their confidence?

Careful What You Reach For

How did I live out last week's Gospel message? What was tough? What was rewarding?

After he had fed the people, Jesus made the disciples get into a boat and precede him to the other side, while he dismissed the crowds. After doing so, he went up on the mountain by himself to pray. When it was evening he was there alone. Meanwhile the boat, already a few miles offshore, was being tossed about by the waves, for the wind was against it. During the fourth watch of the night, he came toward them walking on the sea. When the disciples saw him walking on the sea they were terrified. "It is a ghost," they said, and they cried out in fear. At once Jesus spoke to them, "Take courage, it is I; do not be afraid." Peter said to him in reply, "Lord, if it is you, command me to come to you on the water." He said, "Come." Peter got out of the boat and began to walk on the water toward Jesus. But when he saw how strong the wind was he became frightened; and, beginning to sink, he cried out, "Lord, save me!" Immediately Jesus stretched out his hand and caught Peter, and said to him, "O you of little faith, why did you doubt?" After they got into the boat, the wind died down. Those who were in the boat did him homage, saying, "Truly, you are the Son of God."

About ten years ago, I met a homeless cocaine addict. His addiction developed when he was a teen. He used cocaine to ease the pain and fear from his abusive home. But the cocaine brought him even worse suffering.

Be careful what you reach for when you are hurting or fearful.

That's an important message from today's Gospel. Peter finds himself sinking in a storm. He reaches out to Jesus, who brings him to safety. We have no control over what storms burst in our lives. But we do have control over who or what we reach for when the storms come. Like Peter, we'll find ourselves sinking if we take our focus off Jesus during those tough times. And like the homeless addict I met, we might make mistakes that hurt us for years to come.

Teens are vulnerable to a lot of storms—pain and hurt they just can't avoid or control. Many live in abusive homes or with alcoholic parents. Many suffer in poverty. Many hurt from friends who betray them. Many feel unyielding pressure from parents, teachers, or coaches to excel.

If any of that is true for you, reach out to Jesus for help. Turn away from some things others might choose, like isolation, cutting, drugs, sex, or violence. Strengthen your prayer life. Don't miss Mass. Talk to a priest or Christian counselor. Open up at youth group. Like Peter, you'll find Jesus offering you strength, peace, and a way to safety.

Take :10 Reflect

If a word or phrase from the Gospel grabs your heart, sit quietly for several minutes, repeating it to yourself and asking God to show you how it applies to your life. Or, reflect and possibly journal on the following questions:

- What do you reach for when you face the storms in your life? Does it help you meet your troubles or just ignore them?

Stubborn Like Jesus?

Take :05 Examine

How did I live out last week's Gospel message? What was
tough? What was rewarding?

Take :05 Read

*At that time, Jesus withdrew to the region of Tyre and Sidon.
And behold, a Canaanite woman of that district came and called
out, "Have pity on me, Lord, Son of David! My daughter is
tormented by a demon." But Jesus did not say a word in answer
to her. Jesus' disciples came and asked him, "Send her away, for
she keeps calling out after us." He said in reply, "I was sent only
to the lost sheep of the house of Israel." But the woman came
and did Jesus homage, saying, "Lord, help me." He said in reply,
"It is not right to take the food of the children and throw it to
the dogs." She said, "Please, Lord, for even the dogs eat the
scraps that fall from the table of their masters." Then Jesus said
to her in reply, "O woman, great is your faith! Let it be done for
you as you wish." And the woman's daughter was healed from
that hour.*

"No way, I'm not going. That's not me."

I've heard this often from teens I've invited to retreats
or service trips. But a funny thing almost always happens to
the ones who eventually give in. They go, come back thank-
ful, and want to help with future trips.

We humans can be stubborn. We can think we know
ourselves so well. We sometimes need people to pester us
until we open our minds and reconsider our values or
goals.

We're just like Jesus in this week's Gospel.

I love this story. Jesus seems stubborn and closed-minded, although there may be more going on in the story than we know about. He seems entirely focused on his mission to the Jews—until the Canaanite woman urges him to reconsider. Some Scripture scholars argue that this story really does reflect how Jesus learned about his mission from others who challenged him.

He was fully human. Like us, he had to learn about himself and his talents. It also took him time to understand God's role for him. He didn't know all of this from birth.

Here's the challenge for us. If Jesus needed others to help him learn more about himself, don't we? Think about that this week. When someone disagrees with you, don't be stubborn. Listen. Don't be defensive when someone challenges you. Look within. Don't turn down the opportunity to try new retreats, youth groups, or service trips. Open your mind and go.

Quite often, God calls us to be the people we're called to be—and leads us to the fulfilling life planned for us—through others who disagree, challenge, or invite us. Keep your eyes and ears open this week. A "Canaanite woman" just might come across your path.

Take :10 Reflect

If a word or phrase from the Gospel grabs your heart, sit quietly for several minutes, repeating it to yourself and asking God to show you how it applies to your life. Or, reflect and possibly journal on the following question:

- Who has helped you grow closer to God through an invitation or challenge?

Falling Rocks at Times, but Still Rocks

Take :05 Examine

How did I live out last week's Gospel message? What was tough? What was rewarding?

Take :05 Read

Jesus went into the region of Caesarea Philippi and he asked his disciples, "Who do people say that the Son of Man is?" They replied, "Some say John the Baptist, others Elijah, still others Jeremiah or one of the prophets." He said to them, "But who do you say that I am?" Simon Peter said in reply, "You are the Christ, the Son of the living God." Jesus said to him in reply, "Blessed are you, Simon son of Jonah. For flesh and blood has not revealed this to you, but my heavenly Father. And so I say to you, you are Peter, and upon this rock I will build my church, and the gates of the netherworld shall not prevail against it. I will give you the keys to the kingdom of heaven. Whatever you bind on earth shall be bound in heaven; and whatever you loose on earth shall be loosed in heaven." Then he strictly ordered his disciples to tell no one that he was the Christ.

Some rock, that Peter.

A couple weeks ago, we read how he almost drowned in a storm because he lacked faith. In Holy Week we read about how he denied knowing Jesus—his close friend—to three people to save his skin.

And this week Jesus tells us that this guy will be the rock upon which he builds his Church?

Great news for us!

I don't know about you, but I've got Peter beaten. There have been plenty of times when I've reached out for the wrong things to help me through life's storms. I've also betrayed friends through selfishness or cruel remarks. I've even betrayed myself by going against my values to fit in. In addition, I've let fear keep me from doing the right thing.

It's good to know Jesus can use me as a rock for the Church, despite all that. Yeah, so we're falling rocks at times. But we have a God who looks beyond our mistakes and focuses on our potential.

Look, too many people give up on themselves because they see their sinfulness. God sees all those sins. But Matthew, through this story, tells us that God still chooses us to build a Reign of peace and justice in this world. Peter led the early Church. He was our first pope—despite his flaws. And God has the same faith in you that Jesus had in Peter.

This week be a rock for the people of God's Church around you. Do your best to forgive and reach out. Try living as honestly as possible. Make an effort to put others first. When you mess up, which you probably will, don't get down on yourself. Pray for forgiveness, wisdom, and strength. Remember Peter. Have faith in yourself. And just try again.

Take :10 Reflect

If a word or phrase from the Gospel grabs your heart, sit quietly for several minutes, repeating it to yourself and asking God to show you how it applies to your life. Or, reflect and possibly journal on the following question:

- What causes you to doubt your ability to be a Christian leader?

Find the Honor in Shame

Take :05 Examine

How did I live out last week's Gospel message? What was tough? What was rewarding?

Take :05 Read

Jesus began to show his disciples that he must go to Jerusalem and suffer greatly from the elders, the chief priests, and the scribes, and be killed and on the third day be raised. Then Peter took Jesus aside and began to rebuke him, "God forbid, Lord! No such thing shall ever happen to you." He turned and said to Peter, "Get behind me, Satan! You are an obstacle to me. You are thinking not as God does, but as human beings do."

Then Jesus said to his disciples, "Whoever wishes to come after me must deny himself, take up his cross, and follow me. For whoever wishes to save his life will lose it, but whoever loses his life for my sake will find it. What profit would there be for one to gain the whole world and forfeit his life? Or what can one give in exchange for his life? For the Son of Man will come with his angels in his Father's glory, and then he will repay all according to his conduct."

A few years ago, three teens were shot near my church by another teen who probably thought he was doing the honorable thing.

How did we get here—where violence and revenge, even murder, have become "honorable"?

I've heard it all too often. You can't back down from a fight—you have to get back. Or hazing is okay—you can humiliate a new teammate because you were humiliated when you joined the team.

We still have so much to learn from Jesus and this week's Gospel. The cross was a symbol of shame in the time of Jesus and the early Christians. That's why Jesus' prediction about his death shocks Peter. What a loss of honor for Peter to follow a teacher who would accept a shameful death.

But God transformed the cross from a symbol of shame to a symbol of honor. And God honors those who bear a cross by forgoing vengeance or violence by forgiving and respecting even the people who hurt them.

I know you pay a price when you bear those crosses. It hurts when others put you down, call you names, or laugh behind your back. Jesus is right, however, when he says the pain is worth it. When you go against people who urge you to defend your honor by hurting others, you might lose those friends. Losing them might be like losing a part of your life. But you'll gain so much more.

Each time you stand with Jesus and pick up that cross, you build inner strength. You break free from those who want to control your actions. Each time you do something others think is crazy because you think it is right, you shine more light into a world darkened by sin.

And when it comes down to it, wouldn't you prefer to be honored by God?

Take :10 Reflect

If a word or phrase from the Gospel grabs your heart, sit quietly for several minutes, repeating it to yourself and asking God to show you how it applies to your life. Or, reflect and possibly journal on the following question:

- When have you felt pressured to do something wrong to protect your honor?

Loosen Those Bonds

Take :05 Examine

How did I live out last week's Gospel message? What was tough? What was rewarding?

Take :05 Read

Jesus said to his disciples: "If your brother sins against you, go and tell him his fault between you and him alone. If he listens to you, you have won over your brother. If he does not listen, take one or two others along with you, so that 'every fact may be established on the testimony of two or three witnesses.' If he refuses to listen to them, tell the church. If he refuses to listen even to the church, then treat him as you would a Gentile or a tax collector. Amen, I say to you, whatever you bind on earth shall be bound in heaven, and whatever you loose on earth shall be loosed in heaven. Again, amen, I say to you, if two of you agree on earth about anything for which they are to pray, it shall be granted to them by my heavenly Father. For where two or three are gathered together in my name, there am I in the midst of them."

I was in a car with a teen one day as she poured out her anger about a friend at school.

"Have you talked with him?" I asked.

"He won't listen to me if I try," she responded.

And she just stayed angry and hurt.

Too many people sit in pain and anger after an argument—or after they hear that someone has publicly dissed them. That pain and that anger bind us. They eat up our energy, keep us from focusing on school or work, and make us toss and turn at night.

In this week's Gospel, Jesus offers a recipe for freedom—
confront the person who hurt you.

The early Christians sinned against one another in a variety of
ways. Matthew included this teaching from Jesus, possibly as advice
for them. First, talk about your conflict one on one. If that doesn't
help, find an objective person who might help you work things
out. If that still doesn't work, you might have to end the relationship.

You can use that advice too. When people hurt you, face them
and express your feelings without attacking or insulting them.
Sometimes people don't even know they've done something
hurtful until you confront them. If the people who hurt you won't
listen, look for someone who's objective, maybe an adult, to help
mediate. Sometimes that can help.

Unfortunately, sometimes you'll come across stubborn people
who just can't admit they're wrong. Rather than continue letting
them hurt you, move on to other friendships. You deserve better.

This week resolve to face conflicts head on. As Jesus says,
you'll not only free yourself but you'll also probably be helping the
person who hurt you.

Take :10 Reflect

If a word or phrase from the Gospel grabs your heart, sit quietly
for several minutes, repeating it to yourself and asking God to
show you how it applies to your life. Or, reflect and possibly
journal on the following question:

- How can you find help from Jesus when you need strength to
confront someone who hurts you?

We All Need a Break

Take :05 Examine

How did I live out last week's Gospel message? What was
tough? What was rewarding?

Take :05 Read

*[Jesus said] "The kingdom of heaven may be likened to a king
who decided to settle accounts with his servants. When he began
the accounting, a debtor was brought before him who owed him
a huge amount. Since he had no way of paying it back, his
master ordered him to be sold, along with his wife, his children,
and all his property, in payment of the debt. At that, the servant
fell down, did him homage, and said, 'Be patient with me, and I
will pay you back in full.' Moved with compassion the master of
that servant let him go and forgave him the loan. When that
servant had left, he found one of his fellow servants who owed
him a much smaller amount. He seized him and started to
choke him, demanding, 'Pay back what you owe.' Falling to his
knees, his fellow servant begged him, 'Be patient with me, and I
will pay you back.' But he refused. Instead, he had the fellow
servant put in prison until he paid back the debt. Now when his
fellow servants saw what had happened, they were deeply
disturbed, and went to their master and reported the whole
affair. His master summoned him and said to him, 'You wicked
servant! I forgave you your entire debt because you begged me
to. Should you not have had pity on your fellow servant, as I had
pity on you?' Then in anger his master handed him over to the
torturers until he should pay back the whole debt. So will my
heavenly Father do to you, unless each of you forgives your
brother from your heart." (Matthew 18:23–35)*

Boy, did I almost mess up my ordination.

I spent time planning the ceremony and reception but forgot to reserve the parish hall. When I remembered to book it, the hall was already taken. Luckily, some people helped me correct the problem I caused. The group who had booked the hall even changed their plans for me.

Through it all, everyone was forgiving of my mistake.

I try to remember that mess each time I feel like jumping on someone who makes a mistake that inconveniences me. It helps me calm down, look with compassion, and remember that we all need forgiveness sometimes.

I think that was Jesus' point in this week's Gospel. It hurts when people treat us badly or mess up our day by their mistakes. We can get angry or frustrated. Before we know it, harsh words can fly. That's why it's good to keep our own mistakes in the back of our heads—always slowing us down when we're ready to judge someone else. We just need to give one another a break.

Take :10 Reflect

If a word or phrase from the Gospel grabs your heart, sit quietly for several minutes, repeating it to yourself and asking God to show you how it applies to your life. Or, reflect and possibly journal on the following questions:

- When have you received forgiveness? When have you not offered it?

Never Too Late

Take :05   Examine

How did I live out last week's Gospel message? What was tough? What was rewarding?

Take :05   Read

Jesus told his disciples this parable: "The kingdom of heaven is like a landowner who went out at dawn to hire laborers for his vineyard. After agreeing with them for the usual daily wage, he sent them into his vineyard. Going out about nine o'clock, the landowner saw others standing idle in the marketplace, and he said to them, 'You too go into my vineyard, and I will give you what is just.' So they went off. And he went out again around noon, and around three o'clock, and did likewise. Going out about five o'clock, the landowner found others standing around, and said to them, 'Why do you stand here idle all day?' They answered, 'Because no one has hired us.' He said to them, 'You too go into my vineyard.' When it was evening the owner of the vineyard said to his foreman, 'Summon the laborers and give them their pay, beginning with the last and ending with the first.' When those who had started about five o'clock came, each received the usual daily wage. So when the first came, they thought that they would receive more, but each of them also got the usual wage. And on receiving it they grumbled against the landowner, saying, 'These last ones worked only one hour, and you have made them equal to us, who bore the day's burden and the heat.' He said to one of them in reply, 'My friend, I am not cheating you. Did you not agree with me for the usual daily wage? Take what is yours and go.'" (Matthew 20:1–14a)*

A few years ago, I met a former gang leader who had become a devoted Catholic trying to keep kids out of gangs.

Wow, he came late to the vineyard. But thank God he came.

God's arms never close. At each moment God reaches out to those who've turned away. And as Jesus says this week, God loves people who come late to the vineyard just as much as those who come early.

And those who come late can do awesome ministry. Gang members listened more closely to the former gang leader, because he knew firsthand their struggles. God didn't approve of his former lifestyle but could still use it to spread the Gospel!

The lesson for us? A lot of teens think they've done too much wrong to come home to God. It's just not true. If that's you, know how much God loves you and yearns to draw you close. Also know how much God can use even your mistakes to help other teens who've made bad decisions.

Here's another lesson. Like God, we can't give up on people. We need to be God's representatives—always inviting the people others think are too far gone to change their ways. It is never too late for anyone to come to the vineyard of the Lord.

Take :10 Reflect

If a word or phrase from the Gospel grabs your heart, sit quietly for several minutes, repeating it to yourself and asking God to show you how it applies to your life. Or, reflect and possibly journal on the following question:

• How has God used your past mistakes to help people now?

Our Privilege Is Service

Take :05 Examine

How did I live out last week's Gospel message? What was tough? What was rewarding?

Take :05 Read

Jesus said to the chief priests and elders of the people: "What is your opinion? A man had two sons. He came to the first and said, 'Son, go out and work in the vineyard today.' He said in reply, 'I will not,' but afterwards changed his mind and went. The man came to the other son and gave the same order. He said in reply, 'Yes, sir,' but did not go. Which of the two did his father's will?" They answered, "The first." Jesus said to them, "Amen, I say to you, tax collectors and prostitutes are entering the kingdom of God before you. When John came to you in the way of righteousness, you did not believe him; but tax collectors and prostitutes did. Yet even when you saw that, you did not later change your minds and believe him."

I remember being really frustrated with some young retreat leaders.

They were discussing who should sleep in beds and on the floor during a retreat where beds were limited. The retreat leaders insisted they should get beds, because they were leaders.

Boy, they needed a tongue-lashing from Jesus like the one he gave some Jewish leaders in the reading for this week.

It's normal to want privileges after working hard for a position, whether it's team captain, club president, or retreat leader. But Jesus' followers should always be willing to give up privileges to serve others. Many Jewish religious leaders missed Jesus' message and an opportunity to grow closer to God, because they valued their privileges. Like the older son in the story, they said yes to God but then didn't do the work God asked of them. They closed their minds to Jesus' message and clung to their power. They rejected Jesus' message to change the system that gave them privileges and power over people.

As Christian leaders we need to keep our minds open, even when ideas threaten our egos, our privileges, or our status. Jesus calls us to focus on what's best for the people who look up to us. Can you do that this week when you deal with little brothers and sisters? Can you do it at band or team practice? during that club or youth group meeting?

Sure, privileges are nice, but the greatest privilege is to follow Jesus. This week let's make sure we aren't like the first son. Let's say yes to Jesus' invitation and then set the example for others that he would set.

Take :10 Reflect

If a word or phrase from the Gospel grabs your heart, sit quietly for several minutes, repeating it to yourself and asking God to show you how it applies to your life. Or, reflect and possibly journal on the following question:

- When have the privileges of leadership or being an older sibling tempted you to take advantage of or ignore others?

Heed the Warnings

Take :05 Examine

How did I live out last week's Gospel message? What was tough? What was rewarding?

Take :05 Read

Jesus said to the chief priests and the elders of the people: "Hear another parable. There was a landowner who planted a vineyard, put a hedge around it, dug a wine press in it, and built a tower. Then he leased it to tenants and went on a journey. When vintage time drew near, he sent his servants to the tenants to obtain his produce. But the tenants seized the servants and one they beat, another they killed, and a third they stoned. Again he sent other servants, more numerous than the first ones, but they treated them in the same way. Finally, he sent his son to them, thinking, 'They will respect my son.' But when the tenants saw the son, they said to one another, 'This is the heir. Come, let us kill him and acquire his inheritance.' They seized him, threw him out of the vineyard, and killed him. What will the owner of the vineyard do to those tenants when he comes?" They answered him, "He will put those wretched men to a wretched death and lease his vineyard to other tenants who will give him the produce at the proper times." Jesus said to them, "Did you never read in the Scriptures:

The stone that the builders rejected
    has become the cornerstone;
by the Lord has this been done,
    and it is wonderful in our eyes?

Therefore, I say to you, the kingdom of God will be taken away from you and given to a people that will produce its fruit."

John had had plenty of warnings; he just didn't pay attention.

His mom was alcoholic. He knew that made him more likely to develop a drinking problem. As he started experimenting with alcohol, teachers and ministers warned him that he was heading down the wrong path. At one point he even sat in my office with a friend and talked about giving up alcohol.

Unfortunately, he didn't. By senior year his drinking had ruined his school reputation and made a mess of his life. I pray that he's living a sober life today. But I worry.

God worries about us. God tries to warn us when we're heading down a path that can hurt us or others. Jesus tells a parable this week about all the warnings God has sent through the ages. Many of God's warnings came through prophets who challenged Israel to end poverty and injustice. Often, religious leaders ignored the prophets' warnings and even killed the prophets.

God warns people today in a variety of ways—through concerned friends, through parents who offer discipline, through adult Christians who counsel or challenge us, through God's holy word, which calls us to turn from sin. Are your ears open?

Take :10 Reflect

If a word or phrase from the Gospel grabs your heart, sit quietly for several minutes, repeating it to yourself and asking God to show you how it applies to your life. Or, reflect and possibly journal on the following question:

- How has God warned you through other people that you needed to make a change in your life?

Don't Miss the Invite

Take :05 Examine

How did I live out last week's Gospel message? What was tough? What was rewarding?

Take :05 Read

Jesus again in reply spoke to the chief priests and elders of the people in parables, saying, "The kingdom of heaven may be likened to a king who gave a wedding feast for his son. He dispatched his servants to summon the invited guests to the feast, but they refused to come. A second time he sent other servants, saying, 'Tell those invited: "Behold, I have prepared my banquet, my calves and fattened cattle are killed, and everything is ready; come to the feast."'" Some ignored the invitation and went away, one to his farm, another to his business. The rest laid hold of his servants, mistreated them, and killed them. The king was enraged and sent his troops, destroyed those murderers, and burned their city. Then he said to his servants, 'The feast is ready, but those who were invited were not worthy to come. Go out, therefore, into the main roads and invite to the feast whomever you find.' The servants went out into the streets and gathered all they found, bad and good alike, and the hall was filled with guests." (Matthew 22:1–10)

I remember how much it hurt.

I was in high school and a friend told me that I was not invited to hang out at his place because another person, who didn't like me, didn't want me there.

Rejection. We've all faced it. We've been the last person chosen for a team at recess. We've been ignored at a party. We've sat alone at lunch. A friend has turned on us.

That's why this week's Gospel is such good news. God invites all people to a life full of friendship. Jesus told this parable to criticize religious leaders of his time who rejected his message. Sadly for them, they missed a feast.

Jesus' parable has two more important points. Nothing stops God's party, and he tries to get everyone there.

That's important to remember if life isn't much of a party for you at times, because you're lonely or sad. During those times keep an eye out for God's invitation. It might come through a parent who wants to listen and help. It might come through another teen who invites you to hang out with a different group of people. It might come during prayer, when warmth, peace, and hope soothe the pain that troubles your heart. It might come during that time you spend reading God's word.

But the party is going on. Millions of people worldwide have lives filled with friendship. Millions celebrate daily as they make a difference in the world. Though I struggled with loneliness as a teen, I've found the party now. During those lonely times, don't miss God's invitation.

Take :10 Reflect

If a word or phrase from the Gospel grabs your heart, sit quietly for several minutes, repeating it to yourself and asking God to show you how it applies to your life. Or, reflect and possibly journal on the following question:

- How has God invited you to happiness during times you've felt hurt or lonely?

What Our Nation Really Deserves

Take :05 Examine

How did I live out last week's Gospel message? What was tough? What was rewarding?

Take :05 Read

The Pharisees went off and plotted how they might entrap Jesus in speech. They sent their disciples to him, with the Herodians, saying, "Teacher, we know that you are a truthful man and that you teach the way of God in accordance with the truth. And you are not concerned with anyone's opinion, for you do not regard a person's status. Tell us, then, what is your opinion: Is it lawful to pay the census tax to Caesar or not?" Knowing their malice, Jesus said, "Why are you testing me, you hypocrites? Show me the coin that pays the census tax." Then they handed him the Roman coin. He said to them, "Whose image is this and whose inscription?" They replied, "Caesar's." At that he said to them, "Then repay to Caesar what belongs to Caesar and to God what belongs to God."

A few years ago, an Illinois pharmacist gave up his $100,000-a-year job, because he insisted on giving God what belongs to God—his conscience.

Here's what happened. A state law required all pharmacists to offer a pill that terminates pregnancy. The pharmacist, who believed the pill was a form of abortion, refused to offer it because of his Catholic faith. That cost him his job.

But it saved his conscience—and made other people think.

When is loyalty to Christ more important than loyalty to human laws or even your country? Always, Jesus says in this week's Gospel.

Jesus' enemies question him about his willingness to pay a tax. They hope to trap him. If he opposes the tax, he's liable to arrest. If he supports the tax, he loses support from Jews who hate the Romans. But Jesus' answer makes them take a stand: Give the government what it deserves, and give God what the Lord deserves.

His response has inspired Christians ever since. Dr. Martin Luther King Jr. took his stand in the 1960s by peacefully violating racist laws. U.S. Bishop Thomas Gumbleton took his stand by peacefully protesting our war against Iraq. I remember a student who, as a protest to some U.S. policies, took her stand in the classroom by refusing to stand for the Pledge of Allegiance.

Scripture scholars say the writing on the coin that Jesus examines in this week's Gospel called the Roman emperor "son" of God. But our "Son of God" calls each person to build a world-wide Kingdom where divine laws, not national laws or flags, demand our allegiance.

You might not be old enough to vote. But you still have to pledge your allegiance daily. Our nation deserves citizens who first pledge allegiance to God—and then let that allegiance help shape our nation.

Take :10 Reflect

If a word or phrase from the Gospel grabs your heart, sit quietly for several minutes, repeating it to yourself and asking God to show you how it applies to your life. Or, reflect and possibly journal on the following questions:

- What U.S. laws or policies do you think Jesus would change? Why?

Love and Rules

Take :05 Examine

How did I live out last week's Gospel message? What was tough? What was rewarding?

Take :05 Read

When the Pharisees heard that Jesus had silenced the Sadducees, they gathered together, and one of them, a scholar of the law, tested him by asking, "Teacher, which commandment in the law is the greatest?" He said to him, "You shall love the Lord, your God, with all your heart, with all your soul, and with all your mind. This is the greatest and the first commandment. The second is like it: You shall love your neighbor as yourself. The whole law and the prophets depend on these two commandments."

One of my best friends was a high school principal for many years. I'll always remember one of his rules for teachers: When you doubt whether to discipline a student, show compassion and give the student a break.

He clearly learned from this week's Gospel passage.

In Jesus' time some Pharisees thought Jews could stay close to God by following more than six hundred religious rules. These rules covered everything from eating to bathing. All these rules were considered equally important, and every single one had to be followed. In this week's passage, some Pharisees try to trap Jesus in an argument without a clear answer, perhaps hoping he will say some of the rules aren't as important as others.

But Jesus won't do it. Instead he challenges them to apply all rules in a way that shows their allegiance to the two greatest commandments from the Old Testament: love of God and love of neighbor.

That challenge comes down through the ages to us, as well. Rules are important for a lot of reasons. But my friend the principal was upset when he saw teachers discipline students without showing compassion or respect. As disciples our love must come first, and love must be shown through compassion and respect. Sometimes compassion tells us not to enforce a rule. For example, should a student whose parent just died receive a detention for showing up late for class?

What rules do you enforce? Do you baby-sit for brothers or sisters? Do compassion and respect rule the way you use authority? Are you a team captain? How do you show compassion and respect to new members of the team, especially when humiliating freshmen by hazing them is such a problem in high school sports? Do you lead in a high school club or youth group? Do compassion and respect guide the way you treat peers working on group projects?

This week take a moment to offer a prayer of gratitude. Remember that our God wants to show us compassion and respect, not punishment for breaking the rules. Although we all need to be challenged at times, God knows that people thrive when they feel loved and respected. Let's remember that as we go about enforcing rules.

Take :10 Reflect

If a word or phrase from the Gospel grabs your heart, sit quietly for several minutes, repeating it to yourself and asking God to show you how it applies to your life. Or, reflect and possibly journal on the following question:

- How would God's view of rules affect the way you enforce them? Give a specific example.

There's Only One Perfect Authority

Take :05 Examine

How did I live out last week's Gospel message? What was tough? What was rewarding?

Take :05 Read

Jesus spoke to the crowds and to his disciples, saying, "The scribes and the Pharisees have taken their seat on the chair of Moses. Therefore, do and observe all things whatsoever they tell you, but do not follow their example. For they preach but they do not practice. They tie up heavy burdens hard to carry and lay them on people's shoulders, but they will not lift a finger to move them. All their works are performed to be seen. They widen their phylacteries and lengthen their tassels. They love places of honor at banquets, seats of honor in synagogues, greetings in market-places, and the salutation 'Rabbi.' As for you, do not be called 'Rabbi.' You have but one teacher, and you are all brothers. Call no one on earth your father; you have but one Father in heaven. Do not be called 'Master'; you have but one master, the Christ. The greatest among you must be your servant. Whoever exalts himself will be humbled; but whoever humbles himself will be exalted."

My father made a lot of mistakes as a dad.

For many years that angered me. But in recent years, I've become more forgiving. After a lot of prayer, I've started to realize he could never meet my expectations, because he was human and, therefore, imperfect.

I now realize that I really have only one perfect Father. He's in heaven. That means every father on Earth, and every other authority figure here, deserves a break.

Sometimes we forget that parents, teachers, and religious leaders are limited. They have good and bad days, strengths and weaknesses. This week's Gospel calls us to remember that.

Jesus makes it clear. There is only one perfect Father. This Father is mercy and compassion. This Father will inspire us to greatness and never let us down.

Are you ever too harsh on your parents? Do you ever look at how a religious leader acts and think, "What a hypocrite"?

This week reexamine your expectations of your authority figures and role models. That doesn't mean accepting their verbal or physical abuse. It also doesn't mean that you don't challenge unfair treatment. But ask yourself whether you demand too much. Maybe you also can examine how much time you put into your relationship with our perfect Father in heaven—the one who will help you when others let you down.

Pray too for your parents, religious leaders, teachers, and coaches, asking God to help them in the struggles they face to be good role models.

Take :10 Reflect

If a word or phrase from the Gospel grabs your heart, sit quietly for several minutes, repeating it to yourself and asking God to show you how it applies to your life. Or, reflect and possibly journal on the following question:

* Do you have unrealistic expectations of the authority figures in your life?

Use Your Mistakes as Light for Others

Take :05 Examine

How did I live out last week's Gospel message? What was tough? What was rewarding?

Take :05 Read

Jesus told his disciples this parable: "The kingdom of heaven will be like ten virgins who took their lamps and went out to meet the bridegroom. Five of them were foolish and five were wise. The foolish ones, when taking their lamps, brought no oil with them, but the wise brought flasks of oil with their lamps. Since the bridegroom was long delayed, they all became drowsy and fell asleep. At midnight, there was a cry, 'Behold, the bridegroom! Come out to meet him!' Then all those virgins got up and trimmed their lamps. The foolish ones said to the wise, 'Give us some of your oil, for our lamps are going out.' But the wise ones replied, 'No, for there may not be enough for us and you. Go instead to the merchants and buy some for yourselves.' While they went off to buy it, the bridegroom came and those who were ready went into the wedding feast with him. Then the door was locked. Afterwards the other virgins came and said, 'Lord, Lord, open the door for us!' But he said in reply, 'Amen, I say to you, I do not know you.' Therefore, stay awake, for you know neither the day nor the hour."

Where would I be today, if Father David had not been prepared?

When I was much younger, I had a lot of habits that took me away from Jesus. I partied late on Saturdays and slept late on Sundays. I did a lot that I now regret. I missed a lot of Masses that could have steered me in the right direction.

One day I decided to change these habits but didn't really know where to start. That's when God put Father David into my life. As we talked I discovered that he had made a lot of mistakes like mine when he was young. His efforts to change his life left him with wisdom that helped me. In a way his mistakes lit my path.

He was prepared to help when he was needed. Are you?

This week Jesus advises his followers to prepare themselves. The early Christians thought the world might end at any time. This Gospel challenged them to take an honest, prayerful look at how they were living.

We aren't expecting the world to end soon. But we still need to prepare ourselves the same way. We all make mistakes. We all sin. If we look honestly at those times, repent, and learn from them, then our mistakes and sins can prepare us to help others.

For example, have you made mistakes with alcohol or other drugs? with sex? by being too competitive or too materialistic? Repent, learn from those mistakes, and let them prepare you to help others avoid them.

This week look honestly at your mistakes. Don't be ashamed. Ask God to help you make them lamps that give others light for their lives.

Take :10 Reflect

If a word or phrase from the Gospel grabs your heart, sit quietly for several minutes, repeating it to yourself and asking God to show you how it applies to your life. Or, reflect and possibly journal on the following question:

- When have you used your mistakes to teach others better ways to live?

You *Are* Responsible

Take :05 Examine

How did I live out last week's Gospel message? What was tough? What was rewarding?

Take :05 Read

Jesus told his disciples this parable: "A man going on a journey called in his servants and entrusted his possessions to them. To one he gave five talents; to another, two; to a third, one—to each according to his ability. Then he went away.

"After a long time the master of those servants came back and settled accounts with them. The one who had received five talents came forward bringing the additional five. He said, 'Master, you gave me five talents. See, I have made five more.' His master said to him, 'Well done, my good and faithful servant. Since you were faithful in small matters, I will give you great responsibilities. Come, share your master's joy.'" (Matthew 25:14–15,19–21)

We talk a lot about freedom in the United States but maybe not enough about responsibility. That's why Greg, a former student of mine, made such an impression on me.

As a high school senior, Greg asked to help me at a soup kitchen. He went a few times and saw the difference he made. Within a year he helped start a clothing ministry to homeless people. He kept helping with it after starting college. After college he started working full time with homeless people. Now he also teaches other Catholics how to help people trapped in poverty.

Little by little, as he grew, Greg took on more responsibility. He realized that he could make a difference and that God expected him to do so.

In this week's Gospel, Jesus tells a parable about the landowner who leaves his servants in charge of his possessions. The landowner is grateful to the servants who use the landowners' money (talents) wisely.

In many ways God has left us in charge of his possessions—responsible for the world he created. God also has given us the talents and skills to do that wisely. Freedom is great, but with it comes responsibility to use our talents for others' benefit.

Greg is a good example. In high school he took just a little responsibility for changing the world by going to a soup kitchen. As he grew he realized he could take on more responsibility. So he helped start a ministry. The more he learned about himself, the more he took responsibility for using his freedom to build God's Kingdom.

How do you use your freedom? Believe it or not, you *are* responsible for helping people who are hungry, lonely, put down, or excluded. You *are* responsible for ending violence and vengeance. As a teen start learning how to exercise that responsibility by volunteering—maybe just a little bit at first. Over time you'll see clearly why God trusts you with such enormous responsibility and how much your talents are needed to take care of God's creation.

Take :10 Reflect

If a word or phrase from the Gospel grabs your heart, sit quietly for several minutes, repeating it to yourself and asking God to show you how it applies to your life. Or, reflect and possibly journal on the following question:

• Who inspires you by the way they use their free time to help others?

Jesus Makes Surprising Connections

Take :05 Examine

How did I live out last week's Gospel message? What was tough? What was rewarding?

Take :05 Read

Jesus said to his disciples: "When the Son of Man comes in his glory, and all the angels with him, he will sit upon his glorious throne, and all the nations will be assembled before him. And he will separate them one from another, as a shepherd separates the sheep from the goats. He will place the sheep on his right and the goats on his left. Then the king will say to those on his right, 'Come, you who are blessed by my Father. Inherit the kingdom prepared for you from the foundation of the world. For I was hungry and you gave me food, I was thirsty and you gave me drink, a stranger and you welcomed me, naked and you clothed me, ill and you cared for me, in prison and you visited me.' Then the righteous will answer him and say, 'Lord, when did we see you hungry and feed you, or thirsty and give you drink? When did we see you a stranger and welcome you, or naked and clothe you? When did we see you ill or in prison, and visit you?' And the king will say to them in reply, 'Amen, I say to you, whatever you did for one of the least brothers of mine, you did for me.'" (Matthew 25:31–40)

Many years ago I gave Communion at Mass to a guy I recently had served at a homeless shelter. And this hit me: he and I not only shared the body of Christ, we also were both part of the Body of Christ.

A homeless man and I, part of the same body. It really made me think—just like this week's Gospel.

Christ our king says we serve him when we serve the people considered least in our world. God's Spirit lives in them. God's Spirit also lives in us. Thus, the connection: we are all part of the same body, the Body of Christ.

The child starving in Africa. The kid without friends. The man begging on the street corner. The old person alone. The prisoner serving a sentence. And you and I. All part of the same body.

That means we have to change our thinking at times. When our stomachs hurt, we ask why. We might spend time and money for treatment. We rarely judge or ignore it.

But we sometimes treat parts of our spiritual body—the Body of Christ—differently when they suffer. "I'm too busy to visit," some might say as they pass a nursing home where so many suffer loneliness. "They shouldn't have broken the law," some might say about people in prison.

Our spiritual body stretches around the world. When parts of it suffer, let's take the time to understand why and relieve the pain.

Take :10 Reflect

If a word or phrase from the Gospel grabs your heart, sit quietly for several minutes, repeating it to yourself and asking God to show you how it applies to your life. Or, reflect and possibly journal on the following question:

- What connections or similarities have you seen between yourself and people you've met who are hurting or in need?